HEDDA GABLER

HENRIK IBSEN

Translated by
WILLIAM ARCHER

Translated by
EDMUND GOSSE

CONTENTS

DRAMATIS PERSONAE

GEORGE TESMAN.[1]

HEDDA TESMAN, his wife.

MISS JULIANA TESMAN, his aunt.

MRS. ELVSTED.

JUDGE[2] *BRACK.*

ELIERT LOVBORG.

BERTA, servant at the Tesmans.

The scene of the action is Tesman's villa, in the west end of Christiania.

---

1. *Tesman, whose Christian name in the original is "Jorgen," is described as "stipendiat i kulturhistorie"—that is to say, the holder of a scholarship for purposes of research into the History of Civilisation.*
2. *In the original "Assessor."*

ACT FIRST

SCENE: A spacious, handsome, and tastefully furnished drawing room, decorated in dark colors. In the back, a wide doorway with curtains drawn back, leading into a smaller room decorated in the same style as the drawing-room. In the right-hand wall of the front room, a folding door leading out to the hall. In the opposite wall, on the left, a glass door, also with curtains drawn back. Through the panes can be seen part of a verandah outside, and trees covered with autumn foliage. An oval table, with a cover on it, and surrounded by chairs, stands well forward. In front, by the wall on the right, a wide stove of dark porcelain, a high-backed arm-chair, a cushioned foot-rest, and two footstools. A settee, with a small round table in front of it, fills the upper right-hand corner. In front, on the left, a little way from the wall, a sofa. Further back than the glass door, a piano. On either side of the doorway at the back a whatnot with terra-cotta and majolica ornaments. — Against the back wall of the inner room a sofa, with a table, and one or two chairs. Over the sofa hangs the portrait of a handsome elderly man in a General's uniform. Over the table a hanging lamp, with an opal glass shade. — A number of bouquets are arranged about the drawing-room, in vases and glasses. Others lie upon the tables. The floors in both rooms are covered with thick carpets. — Morning light. The sun shines in through the glass door.

MISS JULIANA TESMAN, with her bonnet on a carrying a parasol, comes in from the hall, followed by BERTA, who carries a bouquet wrapped in paper. MISS TESMAN is a comely and pleasant-looking lady of about sixty-five. She is nicely but simply dressed in a grey walking-costume. BERTA is a middle-aged woman of plain and rather countrified appearance.

Miss Tesman. [*Stops close to the door, listens, and says softly*:] Upon my word, I don't believe they are stirring yet!

Berta. [*Also softly.*] I told you so, Miss. Remember how late the steamboat got in last night. And then, when they got home!—good Lord, what a lot the young mistress had to unpack before she could get to bed.

Miss Tesman. Well well—let them have their sleep out. But let us see that they get a good breath of the fresh morning air when they do appear.

[*She goes to the glass door and throws it open.*

Berta. [Beside the table, at a loss what to do with the bouquet in her hand.] I declare there isn't a bit of room left. I think I'll put it down here, Miss. [*She places it on the piano.*]

Miss Tesman. So you've got a new mistress now, my dear Berta. Heaven knows it was a wrench to me to part with you.

Berta. [*On the point of weeping.*] And do you think it wasn't hard for me, too, Miss? After all the blessed years I've been with you and Miss Rina.[1])

Miss Tesman. We must make the best of it, Berta. There was nothing else to be done. George can't do without you, you see-he absolutely can't. He has had you to look after him ever since he was a little boy.

Berta. Ah but, Miss Julia, I can't help thinking of Miss Rina lying helpless at home there, poor thing. And with only that new girl too! She'll never learn to take proper care of an invalid.

Miss Tesman. Oh, I shall manage to train her. And of course, you know, I shall take most of it upon myself. You needn't be uneasy about my poor sister, my dear Berta.

Berta. Well, but there's another thing, Miss. I'm so mortally afraid I shan't be able to suit the young mistress.

Miss Tesman. Oh well—just at first there may be one or two things—

Berta. Most like she'll be terrible grand in her ways.

Miss Tesman. Well, you can't wonder at that—General Gabler's daughter! Think of the sort of life she was accustomed to in her father's time. Don't you remember how we used to see her riding down the road along with the General? In that long black habit—and with feathers in her hat?

Berta. Yes, indeed—I remember well enough!—But, good Lord, I should never have dreamt in those days that she and Master George would make a match of it.

Miss Tesman. Nor I.—But by-the-bye, Berta—while I think of it: in future you mustn't say Master George. You must say Dr. Tesman.

Berta. Yes, the young mistress spoke of that too—last night—the moment they set foot in the house. Is it true then, Miss?

Miss Tesman. Yes, indeed it is. Only think, Berta—some foreign university has made him a doctor—while he has been abroad, you understand. I hadn't heard a word about it, until he told me himself upon the pier.

Berta. Well well, he's clever enough for anything, he is. But I didn't think he'd have gone in for doctoring people.

Miss Tesman. No no, it's not that sort of doctor he is. [*Nods significantly.*] But let me tell you, we may have to call him something still grander before long.

Berta. You don't say so! What can that be, Miss?

Miss Tesman. [*Smiling.*] H'm—wouldn't you like to know! [*With emotion.*] Ah, dear dear—if my poor brother could only look up from his grave now, and see what his little boy has grown into! [*Looks around.*] But bless me, Berta—why have you done this? Taken the chintz covers off all the furniture.

Berta. The mistress told me to. She can't abide covers on the chairs, she says.

Miss Tesman. Are they going to make this their everyday sitting-room then?

Berta. Yes, that's what I understood—from the mistress. Master George—the doctor—he said nothing.

[*GEORGE TESMAN comes from the right into the inner room, humming to himself, and carrying an unstrapped empty portmanteau. He is a middle-sized, young-looking man of thirty-three, rather stout, with a round, open, cheerful face, fair hair and beard. He wears spectacles, and isS somewhat carelessly dressed in comfortable indoor clothes.]*

Miss Tesman. Good morning, good morning, George.

Tesman. [*In the doorway between the rooms.*] Aunt Julia! Dear Aunt Julia! [*Goes up to her and shakes hands warmly.*] Come all this way—so early! Eh?

Miss Tesman. Why, of course I had to come and see how you were getting on.

Tesman. In spite of your having had no proper night's rest?

Miss Tesman. Oh, that makes no difference to me.

Tesman. Well, I suppose you got home all right from the pier? Eh?

Miss Tesman. Yes, quite safely, thank goodness. Judge Brack was good enough to see me right to my door.

Tesman. We were so sorry we couldn't give you a seat in the carriage. But you saw what a pile of boxes Hedda had to bring with her.

Miss Tesman. Yes, she had certainly plenty of boxes.

Berta. [*To TESMAN*] Shall I go in and see if there's anything I can do for the mistress?

Tesman. No thank you, Berta—you needn't. She said she would ring if she wanted anything.

Berta. [*Going towards the right.*] Very well.

Tesman. But look here—take this portmanteau with you.

Berta. [*Taking it.*] I'll put it in the attic.

[She goes out by the hall door.]

Tesman. Fancy, Auntie—I had the whole of that portmanteau chock full of copies of the documents. You wouldn't believe how much I have picked up from all the archives I have been examining—curious old details that no one has had any idea of—

Miss Tesman. Yes, you don't seem to have wasted your time on your wedding trip, George.

Tesman. No, that I haven't. But do take off your bonnet, Auntie. Look here! Let me untie the strings—eh?

Miss Tesman. [*While he does so.*] Well well—this is just as if you were still at home with us.

Tesman. [*With the bonnet in his hand, looks at it from all sides.*] Why, what a gorgeous bonnet you've been investing in!

Miss Tesman. I bought it on Hedda's account.

Tesman. On Hedda's account? Eh?

Miss Tesman. Yes, so that Hedda needn't be ashamed of me if we happened to go out together.

Tesman. [*Patting her cheek.*] You always think of everything, Aunt Julia. [*Lays the bonnet on a chair beside the table.*] And now, look here— suppose we sit comfortably on the sofa and have a little chat, till Hedda comes.

[*They seat themselves. She places her parasol in the corner of the sofa.*]

Miss Tesman. [*Takes both his hands and looks at him.*] What a delight it is to have you again, as large as life, before my very eyes, George! My George—my poor brother's own boy!

Tesman. And it's a delight for me, too, to see you again, Aunt Julia! You, who have been father and mother in one to me.

Miss Tesman. Oh yes, I know you will always keep a place in your heart for your old aunts.

Tesman. And what about Aunt Rina? No improvement—eh?

Miss Tesman. Oh, no—we can scarcely look for any improvement in her case, poor thing. There she lies, helpless, as she has lain for all these years. But heaven grant I may not lose her yet awhile! For if I did, I don't know what I should make of my life, George—especially now that I haven't you to look after any more.

Tesman. [*Patting her back.*] There there there—!

Miss Tesman. [*Suddenly changing her tone.*] And to think that here are you a married man, George!—And that you should be the one to carry off Hedda Gabler —the beautiful Hedda Gabler! Only think of it —she, that was so beset with admirers!

Tesman. [*Hums a little and smiles complacently.*] Yes, I fancy I have several good friends about town who would like to stand in my shoes—eh?

Miss Tesman. And then this fine long wedding-tour you have had! More than five—nearly six months—

Tesman. Well, for me it has been a sort of tour of research as well. I have had to do so much grubbing among old records—and to read no end of books too, Auntie.

Miss Tesman. Oh yes, I suppose so. [*More confidentially, and lowering her voice a little.*] But listen now, George,—have you nothing—nothing special to tell me?

Tesman. As to our journey?

Miss Tesman. Yes.

Tesman. No, I don't know of anything except what I have told you in my letters. I had a doctor's degree conferred on me—but that I told you yesterday.

Miss Tesman. Yes, yes, you did. But what I mean is—haven't you any —any—expectations—?

Tesman. Expectations?

Miss Tesman. Why you know, George—I'm your old auntie!

Tesman. Why, of course I have expectations.

Miss Tesman. Ah!

Tesman. I have every expectation of being a professor one of these days.

Miss Tesman. Oh yes, a professor—

Tesman. Indeed, I may say I am certain of it. But my dear Auntie— you know all about that already!

Miss Tesman. [*Laughing to herself.*] Yes, of course I do. You are quite right there. [*Changing the subject.*] But we were talking about your journey. It must have cost a great deal of money, George?

Tesman. Well, you see—my handsome travelling-scholarship went a good way.

Miss Tesman. But I can't understand how you can have made it go far enough for two.

Tesman. No, that's not easy to understand—eh?

Miss Tesman. And especially travelling with a lady—they tell me that makes it ever so much more expensive.

Tesman. Yes, of course—it makes it a little more expensive. But Hedda had to have this trip, Auntie! She really had to. Nothing else would have done.

Miss Tesman. No no, I suppose not. A wedding-tour seems to be quite indispensable nowadays.—But tell me now—have you gone thoroughly over the house yet?

Tesman. Yes, you may be sure I have. I have been afoot ever since daylight.

Miss Tesman. And what do you think of it all?

Tesman. I'm delighted! Quite delighted! Only I can't think what we are to do with the two empty rooms between this inner parlour and Hedda's bedroom.

Miss Tesman. [*Laughing.*] Oh my dear George, I daresay you may find some use for them—in the course of time.

Tesman. Why of course you are quite right, Aunt Julia! You mean as my library increases—eh?

Miss Tesman. Yes, quite so, my dear boy. It was your library I was thinking of.

Tesman. I am specially pleased on Hedda's account. Often and often, before we were engaged, she said that she would never care to live anywhere but in Secretary Falk's villa.[2]

Miss Tesman. Yes, it was lucky that this very house should come into the market, just after you had started.

Tesman. Yes, Aunt Julia, the luck was on our side, wasn't it—eh?

Miss Tesman. But the expense, my dear George! You will find it very expensive, all this.

Tesman. [*Looks at her, a little cast down.*] Yes, I suppose I shall, Aunt!

Miss Tesman. Oh, frightfully!

Tesman. How much do you think? In round numbers?—Eh?

Miss Tesman. Oh, I can't even guess until all the accounts come in.

Tesman. Well, fortunately, Judge Brack has secured the most favourable terms for me, so he said in a letter to Hedda.

Miss Tesman. Yes, don't be uneasy, my dear boy.—Besides, I have given security for the furniture and all the carpets.

Tesman. Security? You? My dear Aunt Julia—what sort of security could you give?

Miss Tesman. I have given a mortgage on our annuity.

Tesman. [*Jumps up.*] What! On your—and Aunt Rina's annuity!

Miss Tesman. Yes, I knew of no other plan, you see.

Tesman. [*Placing himself before her.*] Have you gone out of your senses, Auntie? Your annuity—it's all that you and Aunt Rina have to live upon.

Miss Tesman. Well well—don't get so excited about it. It's only a matter of form you know—Judge Brack assured me of that. It was he that was kind enough to arrange the whole affair for me. A mere matter of form, he said.

Tesman. Yes, that may be all very well. But nevertheless—

Miss Tesman. You will have your own salary to depend upon now. And, good heavens, even if we did have to pay up a little—! To eke things out a bit at the start—! Why, it would be nothing but a pleasure to us.

Tesman. Oh Auntie—will you never be tired of making sacrifices for me!

Miss Tesman. [*Rises and lays her hand on his shoulders.*] Have I any other happiness in this world except to smooth your way for you, my dear boy. You, who have had neither father nor mother to depend on. And now we have reached the goal, George! Things have looked black enough for us, sometimes; but, thank heaven, now you have nothing to fear.

Tesman. Yes, it is really marvellous how every thing has turned out for the best.

Miss Tesman. And the people who opposed you—who wanted to bar the way for you—now you have them at your feet. They have fallen, George. Your most dangerous rival—his fall was the worst.—And now he has to lie on the bed he has made for himself—poor misguided creature.

Tesman. Have you heard anything of Eilert? Since I went away, I mean.

Miss Tesman. Only that he is said to have published a new book.

Tesman. What! Eilert Lovborg! Recently—eh?

Miss Tesman. Yes, so they say. Heaven knows whether it can be worth anything! Ah, when your new book appears—that will be another story, George! What is it to be about?

Tesman. It will deal with the domestic industries of Brabant during the Middle Ages.

Miss Tesman. Fancy—to be able to write on such a subject as that!

Tesman. However, it may be some time before the book is ready. I have all these collections to arrange first, you see.

Miss Tesman. Yes, collecting and arranging—no one can beat you at that. There you are my poor brother's own son.

Tesman. I am looking forward eagerly to setting to work at it; especially now that I have my own delightful home to work in.

Miss Tesman. And, most of all, now that you have got the wife of your heart, my dear George.

Tesman. [*Embracing her.*] Oh yes, yes, Aunt Julia! Hedda—she is the best part of it all! I believe I hear her coming—eh?

[*HEDDA enters from the left through the inner room. Her face and figure show refinement and distinction. Her complexion pale and opaque. Her steel-grey eyes express a cold, unruffled repose. Her hair is of an agreeable brown, but not particularly abundant. She is dressed in a tasteful, somewhat loose-fitting morning gown.*]

Miss Tesman. [*Going to meet HEDDA*] Good morning, my dear Hedda! Good morning, and a hearty welcome!

Hedda. [*Holds out her hand.*] Good morning, dear Miss Tesman! So early a call! That is kind of you.

Miss Tesman. [*With some embarrassment.*] Well—has the bride slept well in her new home?

Hedda. Oh yes, thanks. Passably.

Tesman. [*Laughing.*] Passably! Come, that's good, Hedda! You were sleeping like a stone when I got up.

Hedda. Fortunately. Of course one has always to accustom one's self to new surroundings, Miss Tesman—little by little. [Looking towards the left.] Oh, there the servant has gone and opened the veranda door, and let in a whole flood of sunshine.

Miss Tesman. [*Going towards the door.*] Well, then we will shut it.

Hedda. No no, not that! Tesman, please draw the curtains. That will give a softer light.

Tesman. [*At the door.*] All right—all right.—There now, Hedda, now you have both shade and fresh air.

Hedda. Yes, fresh air we certainly must have, with all these stacks of flowers—. But—won't you sit down, Miss Tesman?

Miss Tesman. No, thank you. Now that I have seen that everything is all right here—thank heaven!—I must be getting home again. My sister is lying longing for me, poor thing.

Tesman. Give her my very best love, Auntie; and say I shall look in and see her later in the day.

Miss Tesman. Yes, yes, I'll be sure to tell her. But by-the-bye, George —[Feeling in her dress pocket]—I had almost forgotten—I have something for you here.

Tesman. What is it, Auntie? Eh?

Miss Tesman. [*Produces a flat parcel wrapped in newspaper and hands it to him.*] Look here, my dear boy.

Tesman. [*Opening the parcel.*] Well, I declare!—Have you really saved them for me, Aunt Julia! Hedda! isn't this touching—eh?

Hedda. [*Beside the whatnot on the right.*] Well, what is it?

Tesman. My old morning-shoes! My slippers.

Hedda. Indeed. I remember you often spoke of them while we were abroad.

Tesman. Yes, I missed them terribly. [*Goes up to her.*] Now you shall see them, Hedda!

Hedda. [*Going towards the stove.*] Thanks, I really don't care about it.

Tesman. [*Following her.*] Only think—ill as she was, Aunt Rina embroidered these for me. Oh you can't think how many associations cling to them.

Hedda. [*At the table.*] Scarcely for me.

Miss Tesman. Of course not for Hedda, George.

Tesman. Well, but now that she belongs to the family, I thought—

Hedda. [*Interrupting.*] We shall never get on with this servant, Tesman.

Miss Tesman. Not get on with Berta?

Tesman. Why, dear, what puts that in your head? Eh?

Hedda. [*Pointing.*] Look there! She has left her old bonnet lying about on a chair.

Tesman. [*In consternation, drops the slippers on the floor.*] Why, Hedda—

Hedda. Just fancy, if any one should come in and see it!

Tesman. But Hedda—that's Aunt Julia's bonnet.

Hedda. Is it!

Miss Tesman. [*Taking up the bonnet.*] Yes, indeed it's mine. And, what's more, it's not old, Madam Hedda.

Hedda. I really did not look closely at it, Miss Tesman.

Miss Tesman. [*Trying on the bonnet.*] Let me tell you it's the first time I have worn it—the very first time.

Tesman. And a very nice bonnet it is too—quite a beauty!

Miss Tesman. Oh, it's no such great things, George. [*Looks around her.*] My parasol—? Ah, here. [*Takes it.*] For this is mine too—[*mutters*] — not Berta's.

Tesman. A new bonnet and a new parasol! Only think, Hedda.

Hedda. Very handsome indeed.

Tesman. Yes, isn't it? Eh? But Auntie, take a good look at Hedda before you go! See how handsome she is!

Miss Tesman. Oh, my dear boy, there's nothing new in that. Hedda was always lovely.

[*She nods and goes toward the right.*]

Tesman. [*Following.*] Yes, but have you noticed what splendid condition she is in? How she has filled out on the journey?

Hedda. [*Crossing the room.*] Oh, do be quiet—!

Miss Tesman. [*Who has stopped and turned.*] Filled out?

Tesman. Of course you don't notice it so much now that she has that dress on. But I, who can see—

Hedda. [*At the glass door, impatiently.*] Oh, you can't see anything.

Tesman. It must be the mountain air in the Tyrol—

Hedda. [*Curtly, interrupting.*] I am exactly as I was when I started.

Tesman. So you insist; but I'm quite certain you are not. Don't you agree with me, Auntie?

Miss Tesman. [*Who has been gazing at her with folded hands.*] Hedda is lovely—lovely—lovely. [*Goes up to her, takes her head between both hands, draws it downwards, and kisses her hair.*] God bless and preserve Hedda Tesman—for George's sake.

Hedda. [*Gently freeing herself.*] Oh—! Let me go.

Miss Tesman. [*In quiet emotion.*] I shall not let a day pass without coming to see you.

Tesman. No you won't, will you, Auntie? Eh?

Miss Tesman. Good-bye—good-bye!

[She goes out by the hall door. TESMAN accompanies her. The door remains half open. TESMAN can be heard repeating his message to Aunt Rina and his thanks for the slippers. In the meantime, HEDDA walks about the room, raising her arms and clenching her hands as if in desperation. Then she flings back the curtains from the glass door, and stands there looking out. Presently, TESMAN returns and closes the door behind him.]

Tesman. *[Picks up the slippers from the floor.]* What are you looking at, Hedda?

Hedda. *[Once more calm and mistress of herself.]* I am only looking at the leaves. They are so yellow—so withered.

Tesman. *[Wraps up the slippers and lays them on the table.]* Well, you see, we are well into September now.

Hedda. *[Again restless.]* Yes, to think of it!—already in—in September.

Tesman. Don't you think Aunt Julia's manner was strange, dear? Almost solemn? Can you imagine what was the matter with her? Eh?

Hedda. I scarcely know her, you see. Is she not often like that?

Tesman. No, not as she was to-day.

Hedda. *[Leaving the glass door.]* Do you think she was annoyed about the bonnet?

Tesman. Oh, scarcely at all. Perhaps a little, just at the moment—

Hedda. But what an idea, to pitch her bonnet about in the drawing-room! No one does that sort of thing.

Tesman. Well you may be sure Aunt Julia won't do it again.

Hedda. In any case, I shall manage to make my peace with her.

Tesman. Yes, my dear, good Hedda, if you only would.

Hedda. When you call this afternoon, you might invite her to spend the evening here.

Tesman. Yes, that I will. And there's one thing more you could do that would delight her heart.

Hedda. What is it?

Tesman. If you could only prevail on yourself to say *du*[3] to her. For my sake, Hedda? Eh?

Hedda. No, no, Tesman—you really mustn't ask that of me. I have told you so already. I shall try to call her "Aunt"; and you must be satisfied with that.

Tesman. Well well. Only I think now that you belong to the family, you—

Hedda. H'm—I can't in the least see why—

[*She goes up towards the middle doorway.*]

Tesman. [*After a pause.*] Is there anything the matter with you, Hedda? Eh?

Hedda. I'm only looking at my old piano. It doesn't go at all well with all the other things.

Tesman. The first time I draw my salary, we'll see about exchanging it.

Hedda. No, no—no exchanging. I don't want to part with it. Suppose we put it there in the inner room, and then get another here in its place. When it's convenient, I mean.

Tesman. [*A little taken aback.*] Yes—of course we could do that.

Hedda. [*Takes up the bouquet from the piano.*] These flowers were not here last night when we arrived.

Tesman. Aunt Julia must have brought them for you.

Hedda. [*Examining the bouquet.*] A visiting-card. [*Takes it out and reads:*] "Shall return later in the day." Can you guess whose card it is?

Tesman. No. Whose? Eh?

Hedda. The name is "Mrs. Elvsted."

Tesman. Is it really? Sheriff Elvsted's wife? Miss Rysing that was.

Hedda. Exactly. The girl with the irritating hair, that she was always showing off. An old flame of yours I've been told.

Tesman. [*Laughing.*] Oh, that didn't last long; and it was before I met you, Hedda. But fancy her being in town!

Hedda. It's odd that she should call upon us. I have scarcely seen her since we left school.

Tesman. I haven't see her either for—heaven knows how long. I wonder how she can endure to live in such an out-of-the way hole—eh?

Hedda. [*After a moment's thought, says suddenly.*] Tell me, Tesman— isn't it somewhere near there that he—that—Eilert Lovborg is living?

Tesman. Yes, he is somewhere in that part of the country.

[*BERTA enters by the hall door.*]

Berta. That lady, ma'am, that brought some flowers a little while ago, is here again. [Pointing.] The flowers you have in your hand, ma'am.

Hedda. Ah, is she? Well, please show her in.

[*BERTA opens the door for MRS. ELVSTED, and goes out herself. MRS. ELVSTED is a woman of fragile figure, with pretty, soft features. Her eyes are light blue, large, round, and somewhat prominent, with a startled, inquiring expression. Her hair is remarkably light, almost flaxen, and unusually abundant and wavy. She is a couple of years younger than HEDDA. She wears a dark visiting dress, tasteful, but not quite in the latest fashion.*]

Hedda. [*Receives her warmly.*] How do you do, my dear Mrs. Elvsted? It's delightful to see you again.

Mrs. Elvsted. [*Nervously, struggling for self-control.*] Yes, it's a very long time since we met.

Tesman. [*Gives her his hand.*] And we too—eh?

Hedda. Thanks for your lovely flowers—

Mrs. Elvsted. Oh, not at all—. I would have come straight here yesterday afternoon; but I heard that you were away—

Tesman. Have you just come to town? Eh?

Mrs. Elvsted. I arrived yesterday, about midday. Oh, I was quite in despair when I heard that you were not at home.

Hedda. In despair! How so?

Tesman. Why, my dear Mrs. Rysing—I mean Mrs. Elvsted—

Hedda. I hope that you are not in any trouble?

Mrs. Elvsted. Yes, I am. And I don't know another living creature here that I can turn to.

Hedda. [*Laying the bouquet on the table.*] Come—let us sit here on the sofa—

Mrs. Elvsted. Oh, I am too restless to sit down.

Hedda. Oh no, you're not. Come here.

[*She draws MRS. ELVSTED down upon the sofa and sits at her side.*]

Tesman. Well? What is it, Mrs. Elvsted—?

Hedda. Has anything particular happened to you at home?

Mrs. Elvsted. Yes—and no. Oh—I am so anxious you should not misunderstand me—

Hedda. Then your best plan is to tell us the whole story, Mrs. Elvsted.

Tesman. I suppose that's what you have come for—eh?

Mrs. Elvsted. Yes, yes—of course it is. Well then, I must tell you—if you don't already know—that Eilert Lovborg is in town, too.

Hedda. Lovborg—!

Tesman. What! Has Eilert Lovborg come back? Fancy that, Hedda!

Hedda. Well well—I hear it.

Mrs. Elvsted. He has been here a week already. Just fancy—a whole week! In this terrible town, alone! With so many temptations on all sides.

Hedda. But, my dear Mrs. Elvsted—how does he concern you so much?

Mrs. Elvsted. [*Looks at her with a startled air, and says rapidly.*] He was the children's tutor.

Hedda. Your children's?

Mrs. Elvsted. My husband's. I have none.

Hedda. Your step-children's, then?

Mrs. Elvsted. Yes.

Tesman. [*Somewhat hesitatingly.*] Then was he—I don't know how to express it—was he—regular enough in his habits to be fit for the post? Eh?

Mrs. Elvsted. For the last two years his conduct has been irreproachable.

Tesman. Has it indeed? Fancy that, Hedda!

Hedda. I hear it.

Mrs. Elvsted. Perfectly irreproachable, I assure you! In every respect. But all the same—now that I know he is here—in this great town—and with a large sum of money in his hands—I can't help being in mortal fear for him.

Tesman. Why did he not remain where he was? With you and your husband? Eh?

Mrs. Elvsted. After his book was published he was too restless and unsettled to remain with us.

Tesman. Yes, by-the-bye, Aunt Julia told me he had published a new book.

Mrs. Elvsted. Yes, a big book, dealing with the march of civilisation—in broad outline, as it were. It came out about a fortnight ago. And since it has sold so well, and been so much read—and made such a sensation—

Tesman. Has it indeed? It must be something he has had lying by since his better days.

Mrs. Elvsted. Long ago, you mean?

Tesman. Yes.

Mrs. Elvsted. No, he has written it all since he has been with us—within the last year.

Tesman. Isn't that good news, Hedda? Think of that.

Mrs. Elvsted. Ah yes, if only it would last!

Hedda. Have you seen him here in town?

Mrs. Elvsted. No, not yet. I have had the greatest difficulty in finding out his address. But this morning I discovered it at last.

Hedda. [*Looks searchingly at her.*] Do you know, it seems to me a little odd of your husband—h'm—

Mrs. Elvsted. [*Starting nervously.*] Of my husband! What?

Hedda. That he should send you to town on such an errand—that he does not come himself and look after his friend.

Mrs. Elvsted. Oh no, no—my husband has no time. And besides, I—I had some shopping to do.

Hedda. [*With a slight smile.*] Ah, that is a different matter.

Mrs. Elvsted. [*Rising quickly and uneasily.*] And now I beg and implore you, Mr. Tesman—receive Eilert Lovborg kindly if he comes to you! And that he is sure to do. You see you were such great friends in the old days. And then you are interested in the same studies—the same branch of science—so far as I can understand.

Tesman. We used to be at any rate.

Mrs. Elvsted. That is why I beg so earnestly that you—you too—will keep a sharp eye upon him. Oh, you will promise me that, Mr. Tesman—won't you?

Tesman. With the greatest of pleasure, Mrs. Rysing—

Hedda. Elvsted.

Tesman. I assure you I shall do all I possibly can for Eilert. You may rely upon me.

Mrs. Elvsted. Oh, how very, very kind of you! [*Presses his hands.*] Thanks, thanks, thanks! [*Frightened.*] You see, my husband is so very fond of him!

Hedda. [*Rising.*] You ought to write to him, Tesman. Perhaps he may not care to come to you of his own accord.

Tesman. Well, perhaps it would be the right thing to do, Hedda? Eh?

Hedda. And the sooner the better. Why not at once?

Mrs. Elvsted. [*Imploringly.*] Oh, if you only would!

Tesman. I'll write this moment. Have you his address, Mrs.—Mrs. Elvsted.

Mrs. Elvsted. Yes. [*Takes a slip of paper from her pocket, and hands it to him.*] Here it is.

Tesman. Good, good. Then I'll go in—[*Looks about him.*] By-the-bye,— my slippers? Oh, here. [*Takes the packet and is about to go.*]

Hedda. Be sure you write him a cordial, friendly letter. And a good long one too.

Tesman. Yes, I will.

Mrs. Elvsted. But please, please don't say a word to show that I have suggested it.

Tesman. No, how could you think I would? Eh?

[*He goes out to the right, through the inner room.*]

Hedda. [*Goes up to MRS. ELVSTED, smiles, and says in a low voice.*] There! We have killed two birds with one stone.

Mrs. Elvsted. What do you mean?

Hedda. Could you not see that I wanted him to go?

Mrs. Elvsted. Yes, to write the letter—

Hedda. And that I might speak to you alone.

Mrs. Elvsted. [*Confused.*] About the same thing?

Hedda. Precisely.

Mrs. Elvsted. [*Apprehensively.*] But there is nothing more, Mrs. Tesman! Absolutely nothing!

Hedda. Oh yes, but there is. There is a great deal more—I can see that. Sit here—and we'll have a cosy, confidential chat.

[*She forces MRS. ELVSTED to sit in the easy-chair beside the stove, and seats herself on one of the footstools.*]

Mrs. Elvsted. [*Anxiously, looking at her watch.*] But, my dear Mrs. Tesman—I was really on the point of going.

Hedda. Oh, you can't be in such a hurry.—Well? Now tell me something about your life at home.

Mrs. Elvsted. Oh, that is just what I care least to speak about.

Hedda. But to me, dear—? Why, weren't we schoolfellows?

Mrs. Elvsted. Yes, but you were in the class above me. Oh, how dreadfully afraid of you I was then!

Hedda. Afraid of me?

Mrs. Elvsted. Yes, dreadfully. For when we met on the stairs you used always to pull my hair.

Hedda. Did I, really?

Mrs. Elvsted. Yes, and once you said you would burn it off my head.

Hedda. Oh that was all nonsense, of course.

Mrs. Elvsted. Yes, but I was so silly in those days.—And since then, too—we have drifted so far—far apart from each other. Our circles have been so entirely different.

Hedda. Well then, we must try to drift together again. Now listen. At school we said *du*[4] to each other; and we called each other by our Christian names—

Mrs. Elvsted. No, I am sure you must be mistaken.

Hedda. No, not at all! I can remember quite distinctly. So now we are going to renew our old friendship. [*Draws the footstool closer to Mrs. Elvsted.*] There now! [*Kisses her cheek.*] You must say *du* to me and call me Hedda.

Mrs. Elvsted. [*Presses and pats her hands.*] Oh, how good and kind you are! I am not used to such kindness.

Hedda. There, there, there! And I shall say *du* to you, as in the old days, and call you my dear Thora.

Mrs. Elvsted. My name is Thea.[5]

Hedda. Why, of course! I meant Thea. [Looks at her compassionately.] So you are not accustomed to goodness and kindness, Thea? Not in your own home?

Mrs. Elvsted. Oh, if I only had a home! But I haven't any; I have never had a home.

Hedda. [*Looks at her for a moment.*] I almost suspected as much.

Mrs. Elvsted. [*Gazing helplessly before her.*] Yes—yes—yes.

Hedda. I don't quite remember—was it not as housekeeper that you first went to Mr. Elvsted's?

Mrs. Elvsted. I really went as governess. But his wife—his late wife—was an invalid,—and rarely left her room. So I had to look after the housekeeping as well.

Hedda. And then—at last—you became mistress of the house.

Mrs. Elvsted. [*Sadly.*] Yes, I did.

Hedda. Let me see—about how long ago was that?

Mrs. Elvsted. My marriage?

Hedda. Yes.

Mrs. Elvsted. Five years ago.

Hedda. To be sure; it must be that.

Mrs. Elvsted. Oh those five years—! Or at all events the last two or three of them! Oh, if you[6] could only imagine—

Hedda. [*Giving her a little slap on the hand.*] De? Fie, Thea!

Mrs. Elvsted. Yes, yes, I will try—. Well, if—you could only imagine and understand—

Hedda. [*Lightly.*] Eilert Lovborg has been in your neighbourhood about three years, hasn't he?

Mrs. Elvsted. [*Looks at her doubtfully.*] Eilert Lovborg? Yes—he has.

Hedda. Had you known him before, in town here?

Mrs. Elvsted. Scarcely at all. I mean—I knew him by name of course.

Hedda. But you saw a good deal of him in the country?

Mrs. Elvsted. Yes, he came to us every day. You see, he gave the children lessons; for in the long run I couldn't manage it all myself.

Hedda. No, that's clear.—And your husband—? I suppose he is often away from home?

Mrs. Elvsted. Yes. Being sheriff, you know, he has to travel about a good deal in his district.

Hedda. [*Leaning against the arm of the chair.*] Thea—my poor, sweet Thea—now you must tell me everything—exactly as it stands.

Mrs. Elvsted. Well, then you must question me.

Hedda. What sort of a man is your husband, Thea? I mean—you know—in everyday life. Is he kind to you?

Mrs. Elvsted. [*Evasively.*] I am sure he means well in everything.

Hedda. I should think he must be altogether too old for you. There is at least twenty years' difference between you, is there not?

Mrs. Elvsted. [*Irritably.*] Yes, that is true, too. Everything about him is repellent to me! We have not a thought in common. We have no single point of sympathy—he and I.

Hedda. But is he not fond of you all the same? In his own way?

Mrs. Elvsted. Oh I really don't know. I think he regards me simply as a useful property. And then it doesn't cost much to keep me. I am not expensive.

Hedda. That is stupid of you.

Mrs. Elvsted. [*Shakes her head.*] It cannot be otherwise—not with him. I don't think he really cares for any one but himself—and perhaps a little for the children.

Hedda. And for Eilert Lovborg, Thea?

Mrs. Elvsted. [*Looking at her.*] For Eilert Lovborg? What puts that into your head?

Hedda. Well, my dear—I should say, when he sends you after him all the way to town—[*Smiling almost imperceptibly.*] And besides, you said so yourself, to Tesman.

Mrs. Elvsted. [*With a little nervous twitch.*] Did I? Yes, I suppose I did. [*Vehemently, but not loudly.*] No—I may just as well make a clean breast of it at once! For it must all come out in any case.

Hedda. Why, my dear Thea—?

Mrs. Elvsted. Well, to make a long story short: My husband did not know that I was coming.

Hedda. What! Your husband didn't know it!

Mrs. Elvsted. No, of course not. For that matter, he was away from home himself—he was travelling. Oh, I could bear it no longer, Hedda! I couldn't indeed—so utterly alone as I should have been in future.

Hedda. Well? And then?

Mrs. Elvsted. So I put together some of my things—what I needed most—as quietly as possible. And then I left the house.

Hedda. Without a word?

Mrs. Elvsted. Yes—and took the train to town.

Hedda. Why, my dear, good Thea—to think of you daring to do it!

Mrs. Elvsted. [*Rises and moves about the room.*] What else could I possibly do?

Hedda. But what do you think your husband will say when you go home again?

Mrs. Elvsted. [*At the table, looks at her.*] Back to him?

Hedda. Of course.

Mrs. Elvsted. I shall never go back to him again.

Hedda. [*Rising and going towards her.*] Then you have left your home —for good and all?

Mrs. Elvsted. Yes. There was nothing else to be done.

Hedda. But then—to take flight so openly.

Mrs. Elvsted. Oh, it's impossible to keep things of that sort secret.

Hedda. But what do you think people will say of you, Thea?

Mrs. Elvsted. They may say what they like, for aught *I* care. [*Seats herself wearily and sadly on the sofa.*] I have done nothing but what I had to do.

Hedda. [*After a short silence.*] And what are your plans now? What do you think of doing.

Mrs. Elvsted. I don't know yet. I only know this, that I must live here, where Eilert Lovborg is—if I am to live at all.

Hedda. [*Takes a chair from the table, seats herself beside her, and strokes her hands.*] My dear Thea—how did this—this friendship—between you and Eilert Lovborg come about?

Mrs. Elvsted. Oh it grew up gradually. I gained a sort of influence over him.

Hedda. Indeed?

Mrs. Elvsted. He gave up his old habits. Not because I asked him to, for I never dared do that. But of course he saw how repulsive they were to me; and so he dropped them.

Hedda. [*Concealing an involuntary smile of scorn.*] Then you have reclaimed him—as the saying goes—my little Thea.

Mrs. Elvsted. So he says himself, at any rate. And he, on his side, has made a real human being of me—taught me to think, and to understand so many things.

Hedda. Did he give you lessons too, then?

Mrs. Elvsted. No, not exactly lessons. But he talked to me—talked about such an infinity of things. And then came the lovely, happy time when I began to share in his work—when he allowed me to help him!

Hedda. Oh he did, did he?

Mrs. Elvsted. Yes! He never wrote anything without my assistance.

Hedda. You were two good comrades, in fact?

Mrs. Elvsted. [*Eagerly.*] Comrades! Yes, fancy, Hedda—that is the very word he used!—Oh, I ought to feel perfectly happy; and yet I cannot; for I don't know how long it will last.

Hedda. Are you no surer of him than that?

Mrs. Elvsted. [*Gloomily.*] A woman's shadow stands between Eilert Lovborg and me.

Hedda. [*Looks at her anxiously.*] Who can that be?

Mrs. Elvsted. I don't know. Some one he knew in his—in his past. Some one he has never been able wholly to forget.

Hedda. What has he told you—about this?

Mrs. Elvsted. He has only once—quite vaguely—alluded to it.

Hedda. Well! And what did he say?

Mrs. Elvsted. He said that when they parted, she threatened to shoot him with a pistol.

Hedda. [*With cold composure.*] Oh nonsense! No one does that sort of thing here.

Mrs. Elvsted. No. And that is why I think it must have been that red-haired singing-woman whom he once—

Hedda. Yes, very likely.

Mrs. Elvsted. For I remember they used to say of her that she carried loaded firearms.

Hedda. Oh—then of course it must have been she.

Mrs. Elvsted. [*Wringing her hands.*] And now just fancy, Hedda—I hear that this singing-woman—that she is in town again! Oh, I don't know what to do—

Hedda. [*Glancing towards the inner room.*] Hush! Here comes Tesman. [*Rises and whispers.*] Thea—all this must remain between you and me.

Mrs. Elvsted. [*Springing up.*] Oh yes—yes! For heaven's sake—!

[*GEORGE TESMAN, with a letter in his hand, comes from the right through the inner room.*]

Tesman. There now—the epistle is finished.

Hedda. That's right. And now Mrs. Elvsted is just going. Wait a moment—I'll go with you to the garden gate.

Tesman. Do you think Berta could post the letter, Hedda dear?

Hedda. [*Takes it.*] I will tell her to.

[*BERTA enters from the hall.*]

Berta. Judge Brack wishes to know if Mrs. Tesman will receive him.

Hedda. Yes, ask Judge Brack to come in. And look here—put this letter in the post.

Berta. [*Taking the letter.*] Yes, ma'am.

[*She opens the door for JUDGE BRACK and goes out herself. Brack is a main of forty-five; thick set, but well-built and elastic in his movements. His face is roundish with an aristocratic profile. His hair is short, still almost black, and carefully dressed. His eyebrows thick. His moustaches are also thick, with short-cut ends. He wears a well-cut walking-suit, a little too youthful for his age. He uses an eye-glass, which now and then lets drop.*]

Judge Brack. [*With his hat in his hand, bowing.*] May one venture to call so early in the day?

Hedda. Of course one may.

Tesman. [*Presses his hand.*] You are welcome at any time. [Introducing him.] Judge Brack—Miss Rysing—

Hedda. Oh—!

Brack. [*Bowing.*] Ah—delighted—

Hedda. [*Looks at him and laughs.*] It's nice to have a look at you by daylight, Judge!

Brack. So you find me—altered?

Hedda. A little younger, I think.

Brack. Thank you so much.

Tesman. But what do you think of Hedda—eh? Doesn't she look flourishing? She has actually—

Hedda. Oh, do leave me alone. You haven't thanked Judge Brack for all the trouble he has taken—

Brack. Oh, nonsense—it was a pleasure to me—

Hedda. Yes, you are a friend indeed. But here stands Thea all impatience to be off—so *au revoir* Judge. I shall be back again presently.

[Mutual salutations. MRS. ELVSTED and HEDDA go out by the hall door.]

Brack. Well,—is your wife tolerably satisfied—

Tesman. Yes, we can't thank you sufficiently. Of course she talks of a little re-arrangement here and there; and one or two things are still wanting. We shall have to buy some additional trifles.

Brack. Indeed!

Tesman. But we won't trouble you about these things. Hedda say she herself will look after what is wanting.—Shan't we sit down? Eh?

Brack. Thanks, for a moment. [Seats himself beside the table.] There is something I wanted to speak to about, my dear Tesman.

Tesman. Indeed? Ah, I understand! [Seating himself.] I suppose it's the serious part of the frolic that is coming now. Eh?

Brack. Oh, the money question is not so very pressing; though, for that matter, I wish we had gone a little more economically to work.

Tesman. But that would never have done, you know! Think of Hedda, my dear fellow! You, who know her so well—! I couldn't possibly ask her to put up with a shabby style of living!

Brack. No, no—that is just the difficulty.

Tesman. And then—fortunately—it can't be long before I receive my appointment.

Brack. Well, you see—such things are often apt to hang fire for a long time.

Tesman. Have you heard anything definite? Eh?

Brack. Nothing exactly definite—. [Interrupting himself.] But by-the-bye—I have one piece of news for you.

Tesman. Well?

Brack. Your old friend, Eilert Lovborg, has returned to town.

Tesman. I know that already.

Brack. Indeed! How did you learn it?

Tesman. From that lady who went out with Hedda.

Brack. Really? What was her name? I didn't quite catch it.

Tesman. Mrs. Elvsted.

Brack. Aha—Sheriff Elvsted's wife? Of course—he has been living up in their regions.

Tesman. And fancy—I'm delighted to hear that he is quite a reformed character.

Brack. So they say.

Tesman. And then he has published a new book—eh?

Brack. Yes, indeed he has.

Tesman. And I hear it has made some sensation!

Brack. Quite an unusual sensation.

Tesman. Fancy—isn't that good news! A man of such extraordinary talents—. I felt so grieved to think that he had gone irretrievably to ruin.

Brack. That was what everybody thought.

Tesman. But I cannot imagine what he will take to now! How in the world will he be able to make his living? Eh?

[During the last words, HEDDA has entered by the hall door.]

Hedda. [*To BRACK, laughing with a touch of scorn.*] Tesman is for ever worrying about how people are to make their living.

Tesman. Well you see, dear—we were talking about poor Eilert Lovborg.

Hedda. [*Glancing at him rapidly.*] Oh, indeed? [*Sets herself in the arm-chair beside the stove and asks indifferently:*] What is the matter with him?

Tesman. Well—no doubt he has run through all his property long ago; and he can scarcely write a new book every year—eh? So I really can't see what is to become of him.

Brack. Perhaps I can give you some information on that point.

Tesman. Indeed!

Brack. You must remember that his relations have a good deal of influence.

Tesman. Oh, his relations, unfortunately, have entirely washed their hands of him.

Brack. At one time they called him the hope of the family.

Tesman. At one time, yes! But he has put an end to all that.

Hedda. Who knows? [*With a slight smile.*] I hear they have reclaimed him up at Sheriff Elvsted's—

Brack. And then this book that he has published—

Tesman. Well well, I hope to goodness they may find something for him to do. I have just written to him. I asked him to come and see us this evening, Hedda dear.

Brack. But my dear fellow, you are booked for my bachelor's party this evening. You promised on the pier last night.

Hedda. Had you forgotten, Tesman?

Tesman. Yes, I had utterly forgotten.

Brack. But it doesn't matter, for you may be sure he won't come.

Tesman. What makes you think that? Eh?

Brack. [With a little hesitation, rising and resting his hands on the back of his chair.] My dear Tesman—and you too, Mrs. Tesman—I think I ought not to keep you in the dark about something that —that—

Tesman. That concerns Eilert—?

Brack. Both you and him.

Tesman. Well, my dear Judge, out with it.

Brack. You must be prepared to find your appointment deferred longer than you desired or expected.

Tesman. [*Jumping up uneasily.*] Is there some hitch about it? Eh?

Brack. The nomination may perhaps be made conditional on the result of a competition—

Tesman. Competition! Think of that, Hedda!

Hedda. [*Leans further back in the chair.*] Aha—aha!

Tesman. But who can my competitor be? Surely not—?

Brack. Yes, precisely—Eilert Lovborg.

Tesman. [*Clasping his hands.*] No, no—it's quite impossible! Eh?

Brack. H'm—that is what it may come to, all the same.

Tesman. Well but, Judge Brack—it would show the most incredible lack of consideration for me. [*Gesticulates with his arms.*] For—just think—I'm a married man! We have married on the strength of these prospects, Hedda and I; and run deep into debt; and borrowed money from Aunt Julia too. Good heavens, they had as good as promised me the appointment. Eh?

Brack. Well, well, well—no doubt you will get it in the end; only after a contest.

Hedda. [*Immovable in her arm-chair.*] Fancy, Tesman, there will be a sort of sporting interest in that.

Tesman. Why, my dearest Hedda, how can you be so indifferent about it?

Hedda. [*As before.*] I am not at all indifferent. I am most eager to see who wins.

Brack. In any case, Mrs. Tesman, it is best that you should know how matters stand. I mean—before you set about the little purchases I hear you are threatening.

Hedda. This can make no difference.

Brack. Indeed! Then I have no more to say. Good-bye! [To **Tesman.**] I shall look in on my way back from my afternoon walk, and take you home with me.

Tesman. Oh yes, yes—your news has quite upset me.

Hedda. [*Reclining, holds out her hand.*] Good-bye, Judge; and be sure you call in the afternoon.

Brack. Many thanks. Good-bye, good-bye!

Tesman. [*Accompanying him to the door.*] Good-bye my dear Judge! You must really excuse me—[*JUDGE BRACK goes out by the hall door.*]

Tesman. [*Crosses the room.*] Oh Hedda—one should never rush into adventures. Eh?

Hedda. [*Looks at him, smiling.*] Do you do that?

Tesman. Yes, dear—there is no denying—it was adventurous to go and marry and set up house upon mere expectations.

Hedda. Perhaps you are right there.

Tesman. Well—at all events, we have our delightful home, Hedda! Fancy, the home we both dreamed of—the home we were in love with, I may almost say. Eh?

Hedda. [*Rising slowly and wearily.*] It was part of our compact that we were to go into society—to keep open house.

Tesman. Yes, if you only knew how I had been looking forward to it! Fancy—to see you as hostess—in a select circle! Eh? Well, well, well— for the present we shall have to get on without society, Hedda—only to invite Aunt Julia now and then.—Oh, I intended you to lead such an utterly different life, dear—!

Hedda. Of course I cannot have my man in livery just yet.

Tesman. Oh, no, unfortunately. It would be out of the question for us to keep a footman, you know.

Hedda. And the saddle-horse I was to have had—

Tesman. [*Aghast.*] The saddle-horse!

Hedda. —I suppose I must not think of that now.

Tesman. Good heavens, no!—that's as clear as daylight!

Hedda. [*Goes up the room.*] Well, I shall have one thing at least to kill time with in the meanwhile.

Tesman. [*Beaming.*] Oh thank heaven for that! What is it, Hedda. Eh?

Hedda. [*In the middle doorway, looks at him with covert scorn.*] My pistols, George.

Tesman. [*In alarm.*] Your pistols!

Hedda. [*With cold eyes.*] General Gabler's pistols.

[*She goes out through the inner room, to the left.*]

Tesman. [*Rushes up to the middle doorway and calls after he*r:] No, for heaven's sake, Hedda darling—don't touch those dangerous things! For my sake Hedda! Eh?

---

1. Pronounced Reena.
2. In the original "Statsradinde Falks villa"—showing that it had belonged to the widow of a cabinet minister.
3. *Du* equals thou: Tesman means, "If you could persuade yourself to tutor her."
4. See previous note.
5. Pronounced Tora and Taya.
6. Mrs. Elvsted here uses the formal pronoun De, whereupon Hedda rebukes her. In her next speech Mrs. Elvsted says *du*.

ACT SECOND

SCENE: The room at the TESMANS' as in the first Act, except that the piano has been removed, and an elegant little writing-table with the bookshelves put in its place. A smaller table stands near the sofa on the left. Most of the bouquets have been taken away. MRS. ELVSTED'S bouquet is upon the large table in front.—It is afternoon.

HEDDA, dressed to receive callers, is alone in lhe room. She stands by the open glass door, loading a revolver. The fellow to it lies in an open pistol-case on the writing- table.

Hedda. [*Looks down the garden, and calls*:] So you are here again, Judge!

Brack. [*Is heard calling from a distance.*] As you see, Mrs. Tesman!

Hedda. [*Raises the pistol and points.*] Now I'll shoot you, Judge Brack!

Brack. [*Calling unseen.*] No, no, no! Don't stand aiming at me!

Hedda. This is what comes of sneaking in by the back way.[1] [*She fires*].

Brack. [*Nearer.*] Are you out of your senses—!

Hedda. Dear me—did I happen to hit you?

Brack. [*Still outside.*] I wish you would let these pranks alone!

Hedda. Come in then, Judge.

[JUDGE BRACK, dressed as though for a men's party, enters by the glass door. He carries a light overcoat over his arm.]

33

Brack. What the deuce—haven't you tired of that sport, yet? What are you shooting at?

Hedda. Oh, I am only firing in the air.

Brack. [*Gently takes the pistol out of her hand.*] Allow me, madam! [*Looks at it.*] Ah—I know this pistol well! [*Looks around.*] Where is the case? Ah, here it is. [*Lays the pistol in it, and shuts it.*] Now we won't play at that game any more to-day.

Hedda. Then what in heaven's name would you have me do with myself?

Brack. Have you had no visitors?

Hedda. [*Closing the glass door.*] Not one. I suppose all our set are still out of town.

Brack. And is Tesman not at home either?

Hedda. [*At the writing-table, putting the pistol-case in a drawer which she shuts.*] No. He rushed off to his aunt's directly after lunch; he didn't expect you so early.

Brack. H'm—how stupid of me not to have thought of that!

Hedda. [*Turning her head to look at him.*] Why stupid?

Brack. Because if I had thought of it I should have come a little —earlier.

Hedda. [*Crossing the room.*] Then you would have found no one to receive you; for I have been in my room changing my dress ever since lunch.

Brack. And is there no sort of little chink that we could hold a parley through?

Hedda. You have forgotten to arrange one.

Brack. That was another piece of stupidity.

Hedda. Well, we must just settle down here—and wait. Tesman is not likely to be back for some time yet.

Brack. Never mind; I shall not be impatient.

[*HEDDA seats herself in the corner of the sofa. BRACK lays his overcoat over the back of the nearest chair, and sits down, but keeps his hat in his hand. A short silence. They look at each other.]*

Hedda. Well?

Brack. [*In the same tone.*] Well?

Hedda. I spoke first.

Brack. [*Bending a little forward.*] Come, let us have a cosy little chat, Mrs. Hedda.[2]

Hedda. [*Leaning further back in the sofa.*] Does it not seem like a whole eternity since our last talk? Of course I don't count those few words yesterday evening and this morning.

Brack. You mean since out last confidential talk? Our last *tete-a-tete*?

Hedda. Well yes—since you put it so.

Brack. Not a day passed but I have wished that you were home again.

Hedda. And I have done nothing but wish the same thing.

Brack. You? Really, Mrs. Hedda? And I thought you had been enjoying your tour so much!

Hedda. Oh yes, you may be sure of that!

Brack. But Tesman's letters spoke of nothing but happiness.

Hedda. Oh, Tesman! You see, he thinks nothing is so delightful as grubbing in libraries and making copies of old parchments, or whatever you call them.

Brack. [*With a smile of malice.*] Well, that is his vocation in life—or part of it at any rate.

Hedda. Yes, of course; and no doubt when it's your vocation—. But *I*! Oh, my dear Mr. Brack, how mortally bored I have been.

Brack. [*Sympathetically.*] Do you really say so? In downright earnest?

Hedda. Yes, you can surely understand it—! To go for six whole months without meeting a soul that knew anything of our circle, or could talk about things we were interested in.

Brack. Yes, yes—I too should feel that a deprivation.

Hedda. And then, what I found most intolerable of all—

Brack. Well?

Hedda. —was being everlastingly in the company of—one and the same person—

Brack. [*With a nod of assent.*] Morning, noon, and night, yes—at all possible times and seasons.

Hedda. I said "everlastingly."

Brack. Just so. But I should have thought, with our excellent Tesman, one could—

Hedda. Tesman is—a specialist, my dear Judge.

Brack. Undeniable.

Hedda. And specialists are not at all amusing to travel with. Not in the long run at any rate.

Brack. Not even—the specialist one happens to love?

Hedda. Faugh—don't use that sickening word!

Brack. [*Taken aback.*] What do you say, Mrs. Hedda?

Hedda. [*Half laughing, half irritated.*] You should just try it! To hear of nothing but the history of civilisation, morning, noon, and night—

Brack. Everlastingly.

Hedda. Yes yes yes! And then all this about the domestic industry of the middle ages—! That's the most disgusting part of it!

Brack. [*Looks searchingly at her.*] But tell me—in that case, how am I to understand your—? H'm—

Hedda. My accepting George Tesman, you mean?

Brack. Well, let us put it so.

Hedda. Good heavens, do you see anything so wonderful in that?

Brack. Yes and no—Mrs. Hedda.

Hedda. I had positively danced myself tired, my dear Judge. My day was done—[*With a slight shudder.*] Oh no—I won't say that; nor think it either!

Brack. You have assuredly no reason to.

Hedda. Oh, reasons—[*Watching him closely.*] And George Tesman— after all, you must admit that he is correctness itself.

Brack. His correctness and respectability are beyond all question.

Hedda. And I don't see anything absolutely ridiculous about him. —Do you?

Brack. Ridiculous? N—no—I shouldn't exactly say so—

Hedda. Well—and his powers of research, at all events, are untiring. —I see no reason why he should not one day come to the front, after all.

Brack. [*Looks at her hesitatingly.*] I thought that you, like every one else, expected him to attain the highest distinction.

Hedda. [*With an expression of fatigue.*] Yes, so I did.—And then, since he was bent, at all hazards, on being allowed to provide for me—I really don't know why I should not have accepted his offer?

Brack. No—if you look at it in that light—

Hedda. It was more than my other adorers were prepared to do for me, my dear Judge.

Brack. [*Laughing.*] Well, I can't answer for all the rest; but as for myself, you know quite well that I have always entertained a—a certain respect for the marriage tie—for marriage as an institution, Mrs. Hedda.

Hedda. [*Jestingly.*] Oh, I assure you I have never cherished any hopes with respect to you.

Brack. All I require is a pleasant and intimate interior, where I can make myself useful in every way, and am free to come and go as—as a trusted friend—

Hedda. Of the master of the house, do you mean?

Brack. [*Bowing.*] Frankly—of the mistress first of all; but of course of the master too, in the second place. Such a triangular friendship—if I may call it so—is really a great convenience for all the parties, let me tell you.

Hedda. Yes, I have many a time longed for some one to make a third on our travels. Oh—those railway-carriage *tete-a-tetes*—!

Brack. Fortunately your wedding journey is over now.

Hedda. [*Shaking her head.*] Not by a long—long way. I have only arrived at a station on the line.

Brack. Well, then the passengers jump out and move about a little, Mrs. Hedda.

Hedda. I never jump out.

Brack. Really?

Hedda. No—because there is always some one standing by to—

Brack. [*Laughing.*] To look at your ankles, do you mean?

Hedda. Precisely.

Brack. Well but, dear me—

Hedda. [*With a gesture of repulsion.*] I won't have it. I would rather keep my seat where I happen to be—and continue the *tete-a-tete*.

Brack. But suppose a third person were to jump in and join the couple.

Hedda. Ah—that is quite another matter!

Brack. A trusted, sympathetic friend—

Hedda.—with a fund of conversation on all sorts of lively topics—

Brack.—and not the least bit of a specialist!

Hedda. [*With an audible sigh.*] Yes, that would be a relief indeed.

Brack. [*Hears the front door open, and glances in that direction.*] The triangle is completed.

Hedda. [*Half aloud.*] And on goes the train.

[*GEORGE TESMAN, in a grey walking-suit, with a soft felt hat, enters from the hall. He has a number of unbound books under his arm and in his pockets.*]

Tesman. [*Goes up to the table beside the corner settee.*] Ouf—what a load for a warm day—all these books. [*Lays them on the table.*] I'm positively perspiring, Hedda. Hallo—are you there already, my dear Judge? Eh? Berta didn't tell me.

Brack. [*Rising.*] I came in through the garden.

Hedda. What books have you got there?

Tesman. [*Stands looking them through.*] Some new books on my special subjects—quite indispensable to me.

Hedda. Your special subjects?

Brack. Yes, books on his special subjects, Mrs. Tesman.

[*BRACK and HEDDA exchange a confidential smile.*]

Hedda. Do you need still more books on your special subjects?

Tesman. Yes, my dear Hedda, one can never have too many of them. Of course one must keep up with all that is written and published.

Hedda. Yes, I suppose one must.

Tesman. [*Searching among his books.*] And look here—I have got hold of Eilert Lovborg's new book too. [*Offering it to her.*] Perhaps you would like to glance through it, Hedda? Eh?

Hedda. No, thank you. Or rather—afterwards perhaps.

Tesman. I looked into it a little on the way home.

Brack. Well, what do you think of it—as a specialist?

Tesman. I think it shows quite remarkable soundness of judgment. He never wrote like that before. [*Putting the books together.*] Now I shall take all these into my study. I'm longing to cut the leaves—! And then I must change my clothes. [*To BRACK.*] I suppose we needn't start just yet? Eh?

Brack. Oh, dear no—there is not the slightest hurry.

Tesman. Well then, I will take my time. [*Is going with his books, but stops in the doorway and turns.*] By-the-bye, Hedda—Aunt Julia is not coming this evening.

Hedda. Not coming? Is it that affair of the bonnet that keeps her away?

Tesman. Oh, not at all. How could you think such a thing of Aunt Julia? Just fancy—! The fact is, Aunt Rina is very ill.

Hedda. She always is.

Tesman. Yes, but to-day she is much worse than usual, poor dear.

Hedda. Oh, then it's only natural that her sister should remain with her. I must bear my disappointment.

Tesman. And you can't imagine, dear, how delighted Aunt Julia seemed to be—because you had come home looking so flourishing!

Hedda. [*Half aloud, rising.*] Oh, those everlasting Aunts!

Tesman. What?

Hedda. [*Going to the glass door.*] Nothing.

Tesman. Oh, all right. [*He goes through the inner room, out to the right.*]

Brack. What bonnet were you talking about?

Hedda. Oh, it was a little episode with Miss Tesman this morning. She had laid down her bonnet on the chair there—[*Looks at him and smiles.*]—and I pretended to think it was the servant's.

Brack. [*Shaking his head.*] Now my dear Mrs. Hedda, how could you do such a thing? To the excellent old lady, too!

Hedda. [*Nervously crossing the room.*] Well, you see—these impulses come over me all of a sudden; and I cannot resist them. [*Throws herself down in the easy-chair by the stove.*] Oh, I don't know how to explain it.

Brack. [*Behind the easy-chair.*] You are not really happy—that is at the bottom of it.

Hedda. [*Looking straight before her.*] I know of no reason why I should be—happy. Perhaps you can give me one?

Brack. Well—amongst other things, because you have got exactly the home you had set your heart on.

Hedda. [*Looks up at him and laughs.*] Do you too believe in that legend?

Brack. Is there nothing in it, then?

Hedda. Oh yes, there is something in it.

Brack. Well?

Hedda. There is this in it, that I made use of Tesman to see me home from evening parties last summer—

Brack. I, unfortunately, had to go quite a different way.

Hedda. That's true. I know you were going a different way last summer.

Brack. [*Laughing.*] Oh fie, Mrs. Hedda! Well, then—you and Tesman—?

Hedda. Well, we happened to pass here one evening; Tesman, poor fellow, was writhing in the agony of having to find conversation; so I took pity on the learned man—

Brack. [*Smiles doubtfully.*] You took pity? H'm—

Hedda. Yes, I really did. And so—to help him out of his torment—I happened to say, in pure thoughtlessness, that I should like to live in this villa.

Brack. No more than that?

Hedda. Not that evening.

Brack. But afterwards?

Hedda. Yes, my thoughtlessness had consequences, my dear Judge.

Brack. Unfortunately that too often happens, Mrs. Hedda.

Hedda.

Thanks! So you see it was this enthusiasm for Secretary Falk's villa that first constituted a bond of sympathy between George Tesman and me. From that came our engagement and our marriage, and our wedding journey, and all the rest of it. Well, well, my dear Judge—as you make your bed so you must lie, I could almost say.

Brack. This is exquisite! And you really cared not a rap about it all the time?

Hedda. No, heaven knows I didn't.

Brack. But now? Now that we have made it so homelike for you?

Hedda. Uh—the rooms all seem to smell of lavender and dried rose-leaves.—But perhaps it's Aunt Julia that has brought that scent with her.

Brack. [*Laughing.*] No, I think it must be a legacy from the late Mrs. Secretary Falk.

Hedda. Yes, there is an odour of mortality about it. It reminds me of a bouquet—the day after the ball. [*Clasps her hands behind her head, leans back in her chair and looks at him.*] Oh, my dear Judge—you cannot imagine how horribly I shall bore myself here.

Brack. Why should not you, too, find some sort of vocation in life, Mrs. Hedda?

Hedda. A vocation—that should attract me?

Brack. If possible, of course.

Hedda. Heaven knows what sort of a vocation that could be. I often wonder whether—[*Breaking off.*] But that would never do either.

Brack. Who can tell? Let me hear what it is.

Hedda. Whether I might not get Tesman to go into politics, I mean.

Brack. [*Laughing.*] Tesman? No really now, political life is not the thing for him—not at all in his line.

Hedda. No, I daresay not.—But if I could get him into it all the same?

Brack. Why—what satisfaction could you find in that? If he is not fitted for that sort of thing, why should you want to drive him into it?

Hedda. Because I am bored, I tell you! [After a pause.] So you think it quite out of the question that Tesman should ever get into the ministry?

Brack. H'm—you see, my dear Mrs. Hedda—to get into the ministry, he would have to be a tolerably rich man.

Hedda. [*Rising impatiently.*] Yes, there we have it! It is this genteel poverty I have managed to drop into—! [*Crosses the room.*] That is what makes life so pitiable! So utterly ludicrous!—For that's what it is.

Brack. Now *I* should say the fault lay elsewhere.

Hedda. Where, then?

Brack. You have never gone through any really stimulating experience.

Hedda. Anything serious, you mean?

Brack. Yes, you may call it so. But now you may perhaps have one in store.

Hedda. [*Tossing her head.*] Oh, you're thinking of the annoyances about this wretched professorship! But that must be Tesman's own affair. I assure you I shall not waste a thought upon it.

Brack. No, no, I daresay not. But suppose now that what people call —in elegant language—a solemn responsibility were to come upon you? [Smiling.] A new responsibility, Mrs. Hedda?

Hedda. [*Angrily.*] Be quiet! Nothing of that sort will ever happen!

Brack. [*Warily.*] We will speak of this again a year hence—at the very outside.

Hedda. [*Curtly.*] I have no turn for anything of the sort, Judge Brack. No responsibilities for me!

Brack. Are you so unlike the generality of women as to have no turn for duties which—?

Hedda. [*Beside the glass door.*] Oh, be quiet, I tell you!—I often think there is only one thing in the world I have any turn for.

Brack. [*Drawing near to her.*] And what is that, if I may ask?

Hedda. [*Stands looking out.*] Boring myself to death. Now you know it. [Turns, looks towards the inner room, and laughs.] Yes, as I thought! Here comes the Professor.

Brack. [*Softly, in a tone of warning.*] Come, come, come, Mrs. Hedda!

[*GEORGE TESMAN, dressed for the party, with his gloves and hat in his hand, enters from the right through the inner room.*]

Tesman. Hedda, has no message come from Eilert Lovborg? Eh?

Hedda. No.

Tesman. Then you'll see he'll be here presently.

Brack. Do you really think he will come?

Tesman. Yes, I am almost sure of it. For what you were telling us this morning must have been a mere floating rumour.

Brack. You think so?

Tesman. At any rate, Aunt Julia said she did not believe for a moment that he would ever stand in my way again. Fancy that!

Brack. Well then, that's all right.

Tesman. [*Placing his hat and gloves on a chair on the right.*] Yes, but you must really let me wait for him as long as possible.

Brack. We have plenty of time yet. None of my guests will arrive before seven or half-past.

Tesman. Then meanwhile we can keep Hedda company, and see what happens. Eh?

Hedda. [*Placing BRACK'S hat and overcoat upon the corner settee.*] And at the worst Mr. Lovborg can remain here with me.

Brack. [*Offering to take his things.*] Oh, allow me, Mrs. Tesman!—What do you mean by "At the worst"?

Hedda. If he won't go with you and Tesman.

Tesman. [*Looks dubiously at her.*] But, Hedda dear—do you think it would quite do for him to remain here with you? Eh? Remember, Aunt Julia can't come.

Hedda. No, but Mrs. Elvsted is coming. We three can have a cup of tea together.

Tesman. Oh yes, that will be all right.

Brack. [*Smiling.*] And that would perhaps be the safest plan for him.

Hedda. Why so?

Brack. Well, you know, Mrs. Tesman, how you used to gird at my little bachelor parties. You declared they were adapted only for men of the strictest principles.

Hedda. But no doubt Mr. Lovborg's principles are strict enough now. A converted sinner—[*BERTA appears at the hall door.*]

Berta. There's a gentleman asking if you are at home, ma'am—

Hedda. Well, show him in.

Tesman. [*Softly.*] I'm sure it is he! Fancy that!

[*EILERT LOVBORG enters from the hall. He is slim and lean; of the same age as TESMAN, but looks older and somewhat worn-out. His hair and beard are of a blackish brown, his face long and pale, but with patches of colour on the cheeks. He is dressed in a well-cut black visiting suit, quite new. He has dark gloves and a silk hat. He stops near the door, and makes a rapid bow, seeming somewhat embarrassed.*]

Tesman. [*Goes up to him and shakes him warmly by the hand.*] Well, my dear Eilert—so at last we meet again!

Eilert Lovborg. [*Speaks in a subdued voice.*] Thanks for your letter, Tesman. [*Approaching HEDDA.*] Will you too shake hands with me, Mrs. Tesman?

Hedda. [*Taking his hand.*] I am glad to see you, Mr. Lovborg. [*With a motion of her hand.*] I don't know whether you two gentlemen—?

Lovborg. [*Bowing slightly.*] Judge Brack, I think.

Brack. [*Doing likewise.*] Oh yes,—in the old days—

Tesman. [*To LOVBORG, with his hands on his shoulders.*] And now you must make yourself entirely at home, Eilert! Mustn't he, Hedda?—For I hear you are going to settle in town again? Eh?

Lovborg. Yes, I am.

Tesman. Quite right, quite right. Let me tell you, I have got hold of your new book; but I haven't had time to read it yet.

Lovborg. You may spare yourself the trouble.

Tesman. Why so?

Lovborg. Because there is very little in it.

Tesman. Just fancy—how can you say so?

Brack. But it has been very much praised, I hear.

Lovborg. That was what I wanted; so I put nothing into the book but what every one would agree with.

Brack. Very wise of you.

Tesman. Well but, my dear Eilert—!

Lovborg. For now I mean to win myself a position again—to make a fresh start.

Tesman. [*A little embarrassed.*] Ah, that is what you wish to do? Eh?

Lovborg. [*Smiling, lays down his hat, and draws a packet wrapped in paper, from his coat pocket.*] But when this one appears, George Tesman, you will have to read it. For this is the real book—the book I have put my true self into.

Tesman. Indeed? And what is it?

Lovborg. It is the continuation.

Tesman. The continuation? Of what?

Lovborg. Of the book.

Tesman. Of the new book?

Lovborg. Of course.

Tesman. Why, my dear Eilert—does it not come down to our own days?

Lovborg. Yes, it does; and this one deals with the future.

Tesman. With the future! But, good heavens, we know nothing of the future!

Lovborg. No; but there is a thing or two to be said about it all the same. [*Opens the packet.*] Look here—

Tesman. Why, that's not your handwriting.

Lovborg. I dictated it. [*Turning over the pages.*] It falls into two sections. The first deals with the civilising forces of the future. And here is the second—[*running through the pages towards the end*]— forecasting the probable line of development.

Tesman. How odd now! I should never have thought of writing anything of that sort.

Hedda. [*At the glass door, drumming on the pane.*] H'm—. I daresay not.

Lovborg. [*Replacing the manuscript in its paper and laying the packet on* *the table.*] I brought it, thinking I might read you a little of it this evening.

Tesman. That was very good of you, Eilert. But this evening—? [*Looking back at BRACK.*] I don't see how we can manage it—

Lovborg. Well then, some other time. There is no hurry.

Brack. I must tell you, Mr. Lovborg—there is a little gathering at my house this evening—mainly in honour of Tesman, you know—

Lovborg. [*Looking for his hat.*] Oh—then I won't detain you—

Brack. No, but listen—will you not do me the favour of joining us?

Lovborg. [*Curtly and decidedly.*] No, I can't—thank you very much.

Brack. Oh, nonsense—do! We shall be quite a select little circle. And I assure you we shall have a "lively time," as Mrs. Hed—as Mrs. Tesman says.

Lovborg. I have no doubt of it. But nevertheless—

Brack. And then you might bring your manuscript with you, and read it to Tesman at my house. I could give you a room to yourselves.

Tesman. Yes, think of that, Eilert,—why shouldn't you? Eh?

Hedda. [*Interposing.*] But, Tesman, if Mr. Lovborg would really rather not! I am sure Mr. Lovborg is much more inclined to remain here and have supper with me.

Lovborg. [*Looking at her.*] With you, Mrs. Tesman?

Hedda. And with Mrs. Elvsted.

Lovborg. Ah—[*Lightly.*] I saw her for a moment this morning.

Hedda. Did you? Well, she is coming this evening. So you see you are almost bound to remain, Mr. Lovborg, or she will have no one to see her home.

Lovborg. That's true. Many thanks, Mrs. Tesman—in that case I will remain.

Hedda. Then I have one or two orders to give the servant—

[*She goes to the hall door and rings. BERTA enters. HEDDA talks to her in a whisper, and points towards the inner room. BERTA nods and goes out again.]*

Tesman. [*At the same time, to LOVBORG.*] Tell me, Eilert—is it this new subject—the future—that you are going to lecture about?

Lovborg. Yes.

Tesman. They told me at the bookseller's that you are going to deliver a course of lectures this autumn.

Lovborg. That is my intention. I hope you won't take it ill, Tesman.

Tesman. Oh no, not in the least! But—?

Lovborg. I can quite understand that it must be very disagreeable to you.

Tesman. [*Cast down.*] Oh, I can't expect you, out of consideration for me, to—

Lovborg. But I shall wait till you have received your appointment.

Tesman. Will you wait? Yes but—yes but—are you not going to compete with me? Eh?

Lovborg. No; it is only the moral victory I care for.

Tesman. Why, bless me—then Aunt Julia was right after all! Oh yes—I knew it! Hedda! Just fancy—Eilert Lovborg is not going to stand in our way!

Hedda. [*Curtly.*] Our way? Pray leave me out of the question.

[She goes up towards the inner room, where BERTA is placing a tray with decanters and glasses on the table. HEDDA nods approval, and comes forward again. BERTA goes out.]

Tesman. [*At the same time.*] And you, Judge Brack—what do you say to this? Eh?

Brack. Well, I say that a moral victory—h'm—may be all very fine—

Tesman. Yes, certainly. But all the same—

Hedda. [*Looking at TESMAN with a cold smile.*] You stand there looking as if you were thunderstruck—

Tesman. Yes—so I am—I almost think—

Brack. Don't you see, Mrs. Tesman, a thunderstorm has just passed over?

Hedda. [*Pointing towards the room.*] Will you not take a glass of cold punch, gentlemen?

Brack. [*Looking at his watch.*] A stirrup-cup? Yes, it wouldn't come amiss.

Tesman. A capital idea, Hedda! Just the thing! Now that the weight has been taken off my mind—

Hedda. Will you not join them, Mr. Lovborg?

Lovborg. [*With a gesture of refusal.*] No, thank you. Nothing for me.

Brack. Why bless me—cold punch is surely not poison.

Lovborg. Perhaps not for everyone.

Hedda. I will keep Mr. Lovborg company in the meantime.

Tesman. Yes, yes, Hedda dear, do.

[*He and BRACK go into the inner room, seat themselves, drink punch, smoke cigarettes, and carry on a lively conversation during what follows. EILERT LOVBORG remains standing beside the stove. HEDDA goes to the writing-table.*]

Hedda. [*Raising he voice a little.*] Do you care to look at some photographs, Mr. Lovborg? You know Tesman and I made a tour in the Tyrol on our way home?

[*She takes up an album, and places it on the table beside the sofa, in the further corner of which she seats herself. EILERT LOVBORG approaches, stops, and looks at her. Then he takes a chair and seats himself to her left.*]

Hedda. [*Opening the album.*] Do you see this range of mountains, Mr. Lovborg? It's the Ortler group. Tesman has written the name underneath. Here it is: "The Ortler group near Meran."

Lovborg. [*Who has never taken his eyes off her, says softly and slowly:*] Hedda—Gabler!

Hedda. [*Glancing hastily at him.*] Ah! Hush!

Lovborg. [*Repeats softly.*] Hedda Gabler!

Hedda. [*Looking at the album.*] That was my name in the old days—when we two knew each other.

Lovborg. And I must teach myself never to say Hedda Gabler again—never, as long as I live.

Hedda. [*Still turning over the pages.*] Yes, you must. And I think you ought to practise in time. The sooner the better, I should say.

Lovborg. [*In a tone of indignation.*] Hedda Gabler married? And married to—George Tesman!

Hedda. Yes—so the world goes.

Lovborg. Oh, Hedda, Hedda—how could you[3] throw yourself away!

Hedda. [*Looks sharply at him.*] What? I can't allow this!

Lovborg. What do you mean?

[*TESMAN comes into the room and goes towards the sofa.*

Hedda. [*Hears him coming and says in an indifferent tone.*] And this is a view from the Val d'Ampezzo, Mr. Lovborg. Just look at these peaks! [*Looks affectionately up at TESMAN.*] What's the name of these curious peaks, dear?

Tesman. Let me see. Oh, those are the Dolomites.

Hedda. Yes, that's it!—Those are the Dolomites, Mr. Lovborg.

Tesman. Hedda, dear,—I only wanted to ask whether I shouldn't bring you a little punch after all? For yourself at any rate—eh?

Hedda. Yes, do, please; and perhaps a few biscuits.

Tesman. No cigarettes?

Hedda. No.

Tesman. Very well.

[*He goes into the inner room and out to the right. BRACK sits in the inner room, and keeps an eye from time to time on HEDDA and LOVBORG.*]

Lovborg. [*Softly, as before.*] Answer me, Hedda—how could you go and do this?

Hedda. [*Apparently absorbed in the album.*] If you continue to say *du* to me I won't talk to you.

Lovborg. May I not say *du* even when we are alone?

Hedda. No. You may think it; but you mustn't say it.

Lovborg. Ah, I understand. It is an offence against George Tesman, whom you[4]—love.

Hedda. [*Glances at him and smiles.*] Love? What an idea!

Lovborg. You don't love him then!

Hedda. But I won't hear of any sort of unfaithfulness! Remember that.

Lovborg. Hedda—answer me one thing—

Hedda. Hush! [*TESMAN enters with a small tray from the inner room.*]

Tesman. Here you are! Isn't this tempting? [He puts the tray on the table.

Hedda. Why do you bring it yourself?

Tesman. [*Filling the glasses.*] Because I think it's such fun to wait upon you, Hedda.

Hedda. But you have poured out two glasses. Mr. Lovborg said he wouldn't have any—

Tesman. No, but Mrs. Elvsted will soon be here, won't she?

Hedda. Yes, by-the-bye—Mrs. Elvsted—

Tesman. Had you forgotten her? Eh?

Hedda. We were so absorbed in these photographs. [Shows him a picture.] Do you remember this little village?

Tesman. Oh, it's that one just below the Brenner Pass. It was there we passed the night—

Hedda. —and met that lively party of tourists.

Tesman. Yes, that was the place. Fancy—if we could only have had you with us, Eilert! Eh?

[*He returns to the inner room and sits beside BRACK.*]

Lovborg. Answer me one thing, Hedda—

Hedda. Well?

Lovborg. Was there no love in your friendship for me either? Not a spark—not a tinge of love in it?

Hedda. I wonder if there was? To me it seems as though we were two good comrades—two thoroughly intimate friends. [*Smilingly.*] You especially were frankness itself.

Lovborg. It was you that made me so.

Hedda. As I look back upon it all, I think there was really something beautiful, something fascinating—something daring—in—in that secret intimacy—that comradeship which no living creature so much as dreamed of.

Lovborg. Yes, yes, Hedda! Was there not?—When I used to come to your father's in the afternoon—and the General sat over at the window reading his papers—with his back towards us—

Hedda. And we two on the corner sofa—

Lovborg. Always with the same illustrated paper before us—

Hedda. For want of an album, yes.

Lovborg. Yes, Hedda, and when I made my confessions to you—told you about myself, things that at that time no one else knew! There I would sit and tell you of my escapades—my days and nights of devilment. Oh, Hedda—what was the power in you that forced me to confess these things?

Hedda. Do you think it was any power in me?

Lovborg. How else can I explain it? And all those—those roundabout questions you used to put to me—

Hedda. Which you understood so particularly well—

Lovborg. How could you sit and question me like that? Question me quite frankly—

Hedda. In roundabout terms, please observe.

Lovborg. Yes, but frankly nevertheless. Cross-question me about—all that sort of thing?

Hedda And how could you answer, Mr. Lovborg?

Lovborg. Yes, that is just what I can't understand—in looking back upon it. But tell me now, Hedda—was there not love at the bottom of our friendship? On your side, did you not feel as though you might purge my stains away—if I made you my confessor? Was it not so?

Hedda. No, not quite.

Lovborg. What was you motive, then?

Hedda. Do think it quite incomprehensible that a young girl—when it can be done—without any one knowing—

Lovborg. Well?

Hedda. —should be glad to have a peep, now and then, into a world which—?

Lovborg. Which—?

Hedda. —which she is forbidden to know anything about?

Lovborg. So that was it?

Hedda. Partly. Partly—I almost think.

Lovborg. Comradeship in the thirst for life. But why should not that, at any rate, have continued?

Hedda. The fault was yours.

Lovborg. It was you that broke with me.

Hedda. Yes, when our friendship threatened to develop into something more serious. Shame upon you, Eilert Lovborg! How could you think of wronging your—your frank comrade.

Lovborg. [*Clenches his hands.*] Oh, why did you not carry out your threat? Why did you not shoot me down?

Hedda. Because I have such a dread of scandal.

Lovborg. Yes, Hedda, you are a coward at heart.

Hedda. A terrible coward. [*Changing her tone.*] But it was a lucky thing for you. And now you have found ample consolation at the Elvsteds'.

Lovborg. I know what Thea has confided to you.

Hedda. And perhaps you have confided to her something about us?

Lovborg. Not a word. She is too stupid to understand anything of that sort.

Hedda. Stupid?

Lovborg. She is stupid about matters of that sort.

Hedda. And I am cowardly. [*Bends over towards him, without looking him in the face, and says more softly:*] But now I will confide something to you.

Lovborg. [*Eagerly.*] Well?

Hedda. The fact that I dared not shoot you down—

Lovborg. Yes!

Hedda. —that was not my arrant cowardice—that evening.

Lovborg. [*Looks at her a moment, understands, and whispers passionately.*] Oh, Hedda! Hedda Gabler! Now I begin to see a hidden reason beneath our comradeship! You[5] and I—! After all, then, it was your craving for life—

Hedda. [*Softly, with a sharp glance.*] Take care! Believe nothing of the sort!

[*Twilight has begun to fall. The hall door is opened from without by BERTA.*]

Hedda. [*Closes the album with a bang and calls smilingly:*] Ah, at last! My darling Thea,—come along!

[*MRS. ELVSTED enters from the hall. She is in evening dress. The door is closed behind her.*]

Hedda. [*On the sofa, stretches out her arms towards her.*] My sweet Thea —you can't think how I have been longing for you!

[*MRS. ELVSTED, in passing, exchanges slight salutations with the gentlemen in the inner room, then goes up to the table and gives HEDDA her hand. EILERT LOVBORG has risen. He and MRS. ELVSTED greet each other with a silent nod.*]

Mrs. Elvsted. Ought I to go in and talk to your husband for a moment?

Hedda. Oh, not at all. Leave those two alone. They will soon be going.

Mrs. Elvsted. Are they going out?

Hedda. Yes, to a supper-party.

Mrs. Elvsted. [*Quickly, to LOVBORG.*] Not you?

Lovborg. No.

Hedda. Mr. Lovborg remains with us.

Mrs. Elvsted. [*Takes a chair and is about to seat herself at his side.*] Oh, how nice it is here!

Hedda. No, thank you, my little Thea! Not there! You'll be good enough to come over here to me. I will sit between you.

Mrs. Elvsted. Yes, just as you please.

[*She goes round the table and seats herself on the sofa on HEDDA'S right. LOVBORG re-seats himself on his chair.*]

Lovborg. [*After a short pause, to HEDDA.*] Is not she lovely to look at?

Hedda. [*Lightly stroking her hair.*] Only to look at!

Lovborg. Yes. For we two—she and I—we are two real comrades. We have absolute faith in each other; so we can sit and talk with perfect frankness—

Hedda. Not round about, Mr. Lovborg?

Lovborg. Well—

Mrs. Elvsted. [*Softly clinging close to HEDDA.*] Oh, how happy I am, Hedda! For only think, he says I have inspired him too.

Hedda. [*Looks at her with a smile.*] Ah! Does he say that, dear?

Lovborg. And then she is so brave, Mrs. Tesman!

Mrs. Elvsted. Good heavens—am I brave?

Lovborg. Exceedingly—where your comrade is concerned.

Hedda. Exceedingly—where your comrade is concerned.

Hedda. Ah, yes—courage! If one only had that!

Lovborg. What then? What do you mean?

Hedda. Then life would perhaps be liveable, after all. [*With a sudden change of tone.*] But now, my dearest Thea, you really must have a glass of cold punch.

Mrs. Elvsted. No, thanks—I never take anything of that kind.

Hedda. Well then, you, Mr. Lovborg.

Lovborg. Nor I, thank you.

Mrs. Elvsted. No, he doesn't either.

Hedda. [*Looks fixedly at him.*] But if I say you shall?

Lovborg. It would be of no use.

Hedda. [*Laughing.*] Then I, poor creature, have no sort of power over you?

Lovborg. Not in that respect.

Hedda. But seriously, I think you ought to—for your own sake.

Mrs. Elvsted. Why, Hedda—!

Lovborg. How so?

Hedda. Or rather on account of other people.

Lovborg. Indeed?

Hedda. Otherwise people might be apt to suspect that—in your heart of hearts—you did not feel quite secure—quite confident in yourself.

Mrs. Elvsted. [*Softly.*] Oh please, Hedda—!

Lovborg. People may suspect what they like—for the present.

Mrs. Elvsted. [*Joyfully.*] Yes, let them!

Hedda. I saw it plainly in Judge Brack's face a moment ago.

Lovborg. What did you see?

Hedda. His contemptuous smile, when you dared not go with them into the inner room.

Lovborg. Dared not? Of course I preferred to stop here and talk to you.

Mrs. Elvsted. What could be more natural, Hedda?

Hedda. But the Judge could not guess that. And I say, too, the way he smiled and glanced at Tesman when you dared not accept his invitation to this wretched little supper-party of his.

Lovborg. Dared not! Do you say I dared not?

Hedda. *I* don't say so. But that was how Judge Brack understood it.

Lovborg. Well, let him.

Hedda. Then you are not going with them?

Lovborg. I will stay here with you and Thea.

Mrs. Elvsted. Yes, Hedda—how can you doubt that?

Hedda. [*Smiles and nods approvingly to LOVBORG.*] Firm as a rock! Faithful to your principles, now and for ever! Ah, that is how a man should be! [*Turns to MRS. ELVSTED and caresses her.*] Well now, what did I tell you, when you came to us this morning in such a state of distraction—

Lovborg. [Surprised.] Distraction!

Mrs. Elvsted. [Terrified.] Hedda—oh Hedda—!

Hedda. You can see for yourself! You haven't the slightest reason to be in such mortal terror—[*Interrupting herself.*] There! Now we can all three enjoy ourselves!

Lovborg. [*Who has given a start.*] Ah—what is all this, Mrs. Tesman?

Mrs. Elvsted. Oh my God, Hedda! What are you saying? What are you doing?

Hedda. Don't get excited! That horrid Judge Brack is sitting watching you.

Lovborg. So she was in mortal terror! On my account!

Mrs. Elvsted. [*Softly and piteously.*] Oh, Hedda—now you have ruined everything!

Lovborg. [*Looks fixedly at her for a moment. His face is distorted.*] So that was my comrade's frank confidence in me?

Mrs. Elvsted. [*Imploringly.*] Oh, my dearest friend—only let me tell you—

Lovborg. [*Takes one of the glasses of punch, raises it to his lips, and says in a low, husky voice.*] Your health, Thea!

[*He empties the glass, puts it down, and takes the second.*]

Mrs. Elvsted. [*Softly.*] Oh, Hedda, Hedda—how could you do this?

Hedda. *I* do it? *I*? Are you crazy?

Lovborg. Here's to your health too, Mrs. Tesman. Thanks for the truth. Hurrah for the truth!

[*He empties the glass and is about to re-fill it.*]

Hedda. [*Lays her hand on his arm.*] Come, come—no more for the present. Remember you are going out to supper.

Mrs. Elvsted. No, no, no!

Hedda. Hush! They are sitting watching you.

Lovborg. [*Putting down the glass.*] Now, Thea—tell me the truth—

Mrs. Elvsted. Yes.

Lovborg. Did your husband know that you had come after me?

Mrs. Elvsted. [*Wringing her hands.*] Oh, Hedda—do you hear what his is asking?

Lovborg. Was it arranged between you and him that you were to come to town and look after me? Perhaps it was the Sheriff himself that urged you to come? Aha, my dear—no doubt he wanted my help in his office! Or was it at the card-table that he missed me?

Mrs. Elvsted. [*Softly, in agony.*] Oh, Lovborg, Lovborg—!

Lovborg. [*Seizes a glass and is on the point of filling it.*] Here's a glass for the old Sheriff too!

Hedda. [*Preventing him.*] No more just now. Remember, you have to read your manuscript to Tesman.

Lovborg. [*Calmly, putting down the glass.*] It was stupid of me all this. Thea—to take it in this way, I mean. Don't be angry with me, my dear, dear comrade. You shall see—both you and the others—that if I was fallen once—now I have risen again! Thanks to you, Thea.

Mrs. Elvsted. [*Radiant with joy.*] Oh, heaven be praised—!

[*BRACK has in the meantime looked at his watch. He and TESMAN rise and come into the drawing-room.*]

Brack. [*Takes his hat and overcoat.*] Well, Mrs. Tesman, our time has come.

Hedda. I suppose it has.

Lovborg. [*Rising.*] Mine too, Judge Brack.

Mrs. Elvsted. [*Softly and imploringly.*] Oh, Lovborg, don't do it!

Hedda. [*Pinching her arm.*] They can hear you!

Mrs. Elvsted. [*With a suppressed shriek.*] Ow!

Lovborg. [*To BRACK.*] You were good enough to invite me.

Judge Brack. Well, are you coming after all?

Lovborg. Yes, many thanks.

Brack. I'm delighted—

Lovborg. [*To TESMAN, putting the parcel of MS. in his pocket.*] I should like to show you one or two things before I send it to the printers.

Tesman. Fancy—that will be delightful. But, Hedda dear, how is Mrs. Elvsted to get home? Eh?

Hedda. Oh, that can be managed somehow.

Lovborg. [*Looking towards the ladies.*] Mrs. Elvsted? Of course, I'll come again and fetch her. [*Approaching.*] At ten or thereabouts, Mrs. Tesman? Will that do?

Hedda. Certainly. That will do capitally.

Tesman. Well, then, that's all right. But you must not expect me so early, Hedda.

Hedda. Oh, you may stop as long—as long as ever you please.

Mrs. Elvsted. [*Trying to conceal her anxiety.*] Well then, Mr. Lovborg—I shall remain here until you come.

Lovborg. [*With his hat in his hand.*] Pray do, Mrs. Elvsted.

Brack. And now off goes the excursion train, gentlemen! I hope we shall have a lively time, as a certain fair lady puts it.

Hedda. Ah, if only the fair lady could be present unseen—!

Brack. Why unseen?

Hedda. In order to hear a little of your liveliness at first hand, Judge Brack.

Brack. [*Laughing.*] I should not advise the fair lady to try it.

Tesman. [Also laughing.] Come, you're a nice one Hedda! Fancy that!

Brack. Well, good-bye, good-bye, ladies.

Lovborg. [*Bowing.*] About ten o'clock, then,

[*BRACK, LOVBORG, and TESMAN go out by the hall door. At the same time, BERTA enters from the inner room with a lighted lamp, which she places on the drawing-room table; she goes out by the way she came.*]

Mrs. Elvsted. [*Who has risen and is wandering restlessly about the room.*] Hedda—Hedda—what will come of all this?

Hedda. At ten o'clock—he will be here. I can see him already—with vine-leaves in his hair—flushed and fearless—

Mrs. Elvsted. Oh, I hope he may.

Hedda. And then, you see—then he will have regained control over himself. Then he will be a free man for all his days.

Mrs. Elvsted. Oh God!—if he would only come as you see him now!

Hedda. He will come as I see him—so, and not otherwise! [Rises and approaches THEA.] You may doubt him as long as you please; *I* believe in him. And now we will try—

Mrs. Elvsted. You have some hidden motive in this, Hedda!

Hedda. Yes, I have. I want for once in my life to have power to mould a human destiny.

Mrs. Elvsted. Have you not the power?

Hedda. I have not—and have never had it.

Mrs. Elvsted. Not your husband's?

Hedda. Do you think that is worth the trouble? Oh, if you could only understand how poor I am. And fate has made you so rich! [Clasps her passionately in her arms.] I think I must burn your hair off after all.

Mrs. Elvsted. Let me go! Let me go! I am afraid of you, Hedda!

Berta. [*In the middle doorway.*] Tea is laid in the dining-room, ma'am.

Hedda. Very well. We are coming

Mrs. Elvsted. No, no, no! I would rather go home alone! At once!

Hedda. Nonsense! First you shall have a cup of tea, you little stupid. And then—at ten o'clock—Eilert Lovborg will be here—with vine-leaves in his hair.

[She drags MRS. ELVSTED almost by force to the middle doorway.]

---

1. *Bagveje* means both "back ways" and "underhand courses."
2. As this form of address is contrary to English usage, and as the note of familiarity would be lacking in "Mrs. Tesman," Brack may, in stage representation, say "Miss Hedda," thus ignoring her marriage and reverting to the form of address no doubt customary between them of old.
3. He uses the familiar *du*.
4. From this point onward Lovborg use the formal *De*.
5. In this speech he once more says *du*. Hedda addresses him throughout as *De*.

ACT THIRD

SCENE: The room at the TESMANS'. The curtains are drawn over the middle doorway, and also over the glass door. The lamp, half turned down, and with a shade over it, is burning on the table. In the stove, the door of which stands open, there has been a fire, which is now nearly burnt out.

MRS. ELVSTED, wrapped in a large shawl, and with her feet upon a footrest, sits close to the stove, sunk back in the arm-chair. HEDDA, fully dressed, lies sleeping upon the sofa, with a sofa-blanket over her.

Mrs. Elvsted. [*After a pause, suddenly sits up in her chair, and listens eagerly. Then she sinks back again wearily, moaning to herself.*] Not yet!— Oh God—oh God—not yet!

[*BERTA slips cautiously in by the hall door. She has a letter in her hand.*]

Mrs. Elvsted. [*Turns and whispers eagerly.*] Well—has any one come?

Berta. [*Softly.*] Yes, a girl has just brought this letter.

Mrs. Elvsted. [*Quickly, holding out her hand.*] A letter! Give it to me!

Berta. No, it's for Dr. Tesman, ma'am.

Mrs. Elvsted. Oh, indeed.

Berta. It was Miss Tesman's servant that brought it. I'll lay it here on the table.

Mrs. Elvsted. Yes, do.

Berta. [*Laying down the letter.*] I think I had better put out the lamp. It's smoking.

Mrs. Elvsted. Yes, put it out. It must soon be daylight now.

Berta. [*Putting out the lamp.*] It is daylight already, ma'am.

Mrs. Elvsted. Yes, broad day! And no one come back yet—!

Berta. Lord bless you, ma'am—I guessed how it would be.

Mrs. Elvsted. You guessed?

Berta. Yes, when I saw that a certain person had come back to town—and that he went off with them. For we've heard enough about that gentleman before now.

Mrs. Elvsted. Don't speak so loud. You will waken Mrs. Tesman.

Berta. [*Looks towards the sofa and sighs.*] No, no—let her sleep, poor thing. Shan't I put some wood on the fire?

Mrs. Elvsted. Thanks, not for me.

Berta. Oh, very well. [*She goes softly out by the hall door.*]

Hedda. [*Is wakened by the shutting of the door, and looks up.*] What's that—?

Mrs. Elvsted. It was only the servant.

Hedda. [*Looking about her.*] Oh, we're here—! Yes, now I remember. [*Sits erect upon the sofa, stretches herself, and rubs her eyes.*] What o'clock is it, Thea?

Mrs. Elvsted. [*Looks at her watch.*] It's past seven.

Hedda. When did Tesman come home?

Mrs. Elvsted. He has not come.

Hedda. Not come home yet?

Mrs. Elvsted. [*Rising.*] No one has come.

Hedda. Think of our watching and waiting here till four in the morning—

Mrs. Elvsted. [*Wringing her hands.*] And how I watched and waited for him!

Hedda. [*Yawns, and says with her hand before her mouth.*] Well well—we might have spared ourselves the trouble.

Mrs. Elvsted. Did you get a little sleep?

Hedda. Oh yes; I believe I have slept pretty well. Have you not?

Mrs. Elvsted. Not for a moment. I couldn't, Hedda!—not to save my life.

Hedda. [*Rises and goes towards her.*] There there there! There's nothing to be so alarmed about. I understand quite well what has happened.

Mrs. Elvsted. Well, what do you think? Won't you tell me?

Hedda. Why, of course it has been a very late affair at Judge Brack's—

Mrs. Elvsted. Yes, yes—that is clear enough. But all the same—

Hedda. And then, you see, Tesman hasn't cared to come home and ring us up in the middle of the night. [*Laughing.*] Perhaps he wasn't inclined to show himself either—immediately after a jollification.

Mrs. Elvsted. But in that case—where can he have gone?

Hedda. Of course he has gone to his Aunts' and slept there. They have his old room ready for him.

Mrs. Elvsted. No, he can't be with them for a letter has just come for him from Miss Tesman. There it lies.

Hedda. Indeed? [*Looks at the address.*] Why yes, it's addressed in Aunt Julia's hand. Well then, he has remained at Judge Brack's. And as for Eilert Lovborg—he is sitting, with vine-leaves in his hair, reading his manuscript.

Mrs. Elvsted. Oh, Hedda, you are just saying things you don't believe a bit.

Hedda. You really are a little blockhead, Thea.

Mrs. Elvsted. Oh yes, I suppose I am.

Hedda. And how mortally tired you look.

Mrs. Elvsted. Yes, I am mortally tired.

Hedda. Well then, you must do as I tell you. You must go into my room and lie down for a little while.

Mrs. Elvsted. Oh no, no—I shouldn't be able to sleep.

Hedda. I am sure you would.

Mrs. Elvsted. Well, but you husband is certain to come soon now; and then I want to know at once—

Hedda. I shall take care to let you know when he comes.

Mrs. Elvsted. Do you promise me, Hedda?

Hedda. Yes, rely upon me. Just you go in and have a sleep in the meantime.

Mrs. Elvsted. Thanks; then I'll try. [*She goes off to the inner room.*]

[*HEDDA goes up to the glass door and draws back the curtains. The broad daylight streams into the room. Then she takes a little hand-glass from the writing-table, looks at herself in it, and arranges her hair. Next she goes to the hall door and presses the bell-button. BERTA presently appears at the hall door.*]

Berta. Did you want anything, ma'am?

Hedda. Yes; you must put some more wood in the stove. I am shivering.

Berta. Bless me—I'll make up the fire at once. [*She rakes the embers together and lays a piece of wood upon them; then stops and listens.*] That was a ring at the front door, ma'am.

Hedda. Then go to the door. I will look after the fire.

Berta. It'll soon burn up. [*She goes out by the hall door.*]

[*HEDDA kneels on the foot-rest and lays some more pieces of wood in the stove. After a short pause, GEORGE TESMAN enters from the hall. He steals on tiptoe towards the middle doorway and is about to slip through the curtains.*]

Hedda. [*At the stove, without looking up.*] Good morning.

Tesman. [*Turns.*] Hedda! [*Approaching her.*] Good heavens—are you up so early? Eh?

Hedda. Yes, I am up very early this morning.

Tesman. And I never doubted you were still sound asleep! Fancy that,

Hedda!

Hedda. Don't speak so loud. Mrs. Elvsted is resting in my room.

Tesman. Has Mrs. Elvsted been here all night?

Hedda. Yes, since no one came to fetch her.

Tesman. Ah, to be sure.

Hedda. [*Closes the door of the stove and rises.*] Well, did you enjoy yourselves at Judge Brack's?

Tesman. Have you been anxious about me? Eh?

Hedda. No, I should never think of being anxious. But I asked if you had enjoyed yourself.

Tesman. Oh yes,—for once in a way. Especially the beginning of the evening; for then Eilert read me part of his book. We arrived more than an hour too early—fancy that! And Brack had all sorts of arrangements to make—so Eilert read to me.

Hedda. [*Seating herself by the table on the right.*] Well? Tell me then—

Tesman. [*Sitting on a footstool near the stove.*] Oh, Hedda, you can't conceive what a book that is going to be! I believe it is one of the most remarkable things that have ever been written. Fancy that!

Hedda. Yes yes; I don't care about that—

Tesman. I must make a confession to you, Hedda. When he had finished reading—a horrid feeling came over me.

Hedda. A horrid feeling?

Tesman. I felt jealous of Eilert for having had it in him to write such a book. Only think, Hedda!

Hedda. Yes, yes, I am thinking!

Tesman. And then how pitiful to think that he—with all his gifts—should be irreclaimable, after all.

Hedda. I suppose you mean that he has more courage than the rest?

Tesman. No, not at all—I mean that he is incapable of taking his pleasure in moderation.

Hedda. And what came of it all—in the end?

Tesman. Well, to tell the truth, I think it might best be described as an orgie, Hedda.

Hedda. Had he vine-leaves in his hair?

Tesman. Vine-leaves? No, I saw nothing of the sort. But he made a long, rambling speech in honour of the woman who had inspired him in his work—that was the phrase he used.

Hedda. Did he name her?

Tesman. No, he didn't; but I can't help thinking he meant Mrs. Elvsted. You may be sure he did.

Hedda. Well—where did you part from him?

Tesman. On the way to town. We broke up—the last of us at any rate —all together; and Brack came with us to get a breath of fresh air. And then, you see, we agreed to take Eilert home; for he had had far more than was good for him.

Hedda. I daresay.

Tesman. But now comes the strange part of it, Hedda; or, I should rather say, the melancholy part of it. I declare I am almost ashamed— on Eilert's account—to tell you—

Hedda. Oh, go on—!

Tesman. Well, as we were getting near town, you see, I happened to drop a little behind the others. Only for a minute or two—fancy that!

Hedda. Yes yes yes, but—?

Tesman. And then, as I hurried after them—what do you think I found by the wayside? Eh?

Hedda. Oh, how should I know!

Tesman. You mustn't speak of it to a soul, Hedda! Do you hear! Promise me, for Eilert's sake. [*Draws a parcel, wrapped in paper, from his coat pocket.*] Fancy, dear—I found this.

Hedda. Is not that the parcel he had with him yesterday?

Tesman. Yes, it is the whole of his precious, irreplaceable manuscript!

And he had gone and lost it, and knew nothing about it. Only fancy, Hedda! So deplorably—

Hedda. But why did you not give him back the parcel at once?

Tesman. I didn't dare to—in the state he was then in—

Hedda. Did you not tell any of the others that you had found it?

Tesman. Oh, far from it! You can surely understand that, for Eilert's sake, I wouldn't do that.

Hedda. So no one knows that Eilert Lovborg's manuscript is in your possession?

Tesman. No. And no one must know it.

Hedda. Then what did you say to him afterwards?

Tesman. I didn't talk to him again at all; for when we got in among the streets, he and two or three of the others gave us the slip and disappeared. Fancy that!

Hedda. Indeed! They must have taken him home then.

Tesman. Yes, so it would appear. And Brack, too, left us.

Hedda. And what have you been doing with yourself since?

Tesman. Well, I and some of the others went home with one of the party, a jolly fellow, and took our morning coffee with him; or perhaps I should rather call it our night coffee—eh? But now, when I have rested a little, and given Eilert, poor fellow, time to have his sleep out, I must take this back to him.

Hedda. [*Holds out her hand for the packet.*] No—don't give it to him! Not in such a hurry, I mean. Let me read it first.

Tesman. No, my dearest Hedda, I mustn't, I really mustn't.

Hedda. You must not?

Tesman. No—for you can imagine what a state of despair he will be in when he wakens and misses the manuscript. He has no copy of it, you must know! He told me so.

Hedda. [*Looking searchingly at him.*] Can such a thing not be reproduced? Written over again?

Tesman. No, I don't think that would be possible. For the inspiration, you see—

Hedda. Yes, yes—I suppose it depends on that—[*Lightly.*] But, by-the-bye —here is a letter for you.

Tesman. Fancy—!

Hedda. [*Handing it to him.*] It came early this morning.

Tesman. It's from Aunt Julia! What can it be? [He lays the packet on the other footstool, opens the letter, runs his eye through it, and jumps up.] Oh, Hedda—she says that poor Aunt Rina is dying!

Hedda. Well, we were prepared for that.

Tesman. And that if I want to see her again, I must make haste. I'll run in to them at once.

Hedda. [*Suppressing a smile.*] Will you run?

Tesman. Oh, my dearest Hedda—if you could only make up your mind to come with me! Just think!

Hedda. [*Rises and says wearily, repelling the idea.*] No, no don't ask me. I will not look upon sickness and death. I loathe all sorts of ugliness.

Tesman. Well, well, then—! [*Bustling around.*] My hat—? My overcoat —? Oh, in the hall—. I do hope I mayn't come too late, Hedda! Eh?

Hedda. Oh, if you run—[BERTA *appears at the hall door.*]

Berta. Judge Brack is at the door, and wishes to know if he may come in.

Tesman. At this time! No, I can't possibly see him.

Hedda. But I can. [*To* BERTA.] Ask Judge Brack to come in. [BERTA goes out.

Hedda. [*Quickly, whispering.*] The parcel, Tesman!

[*She snatches it up from the stool.*]

Tesman. Yes, give it to me!

Hedda. No, no, I will keep it till you come back.

[*She goes to the writing-table and places it in the bookcase. TESMAN stands in a flurry of haste, and cannot get his gloves on. JUDGE BRACK enters from the hall.]*

Hedda. [*Nodding to him.*] You are an early bird, I must say.

Brack. Yes, don't you think so! [*To TESMAN.*] Are you on the move, too?

Tesman. Yes, I must rush of to my aunts'. Fancy—the invalid one is lying at death's door, poor creature.

Brack. Dear me, is she indeed? Then on no account let me detain you. At such a critical moment—

Tesman. Yes, I must really rush—Good-bye! Good-bye!

[He hastens out by the hall door.]

Hedda. [*Approaching.*] You seem to have made a particularly lively night of it at your rooms, Judge Brack.

Brack. I assure you I have not had my clothes off, Mrs. Hedda.

Hedda. Not you, either?

Brack. No, as you may see. But what has Tesman been telling you of the night's adventures?

Hedda. Oh, some tiresome story. Only that they went and had coffee somewhere or other.

Brack. I have heard about that coffee-party already. Eilert Lovborg was not with them, I fancy?

Hedda. No, they had taken him home before that.

Brack. Tesman too?

Hedda. No, but some of the others, he said.

Brack. [*Smiling.*] George Tesman is really an ingenuous creature, Mrs. Hedda.

Hedda. Yes, heaven knows he is. Then is there something behind all this?

Brack. Yes, perhaps there may be.

Hedda. Well then, sit down, my dear Judge, and tell your story in comfort.

[She seats herself to the left of the table. BRACK sits near her, at the long side of the table.]

Hedda. Now then?

Brack. I had special reasons for keeping track of my guests—last night.

Hedda. Of Eilert Lovborg among the rest, perhaps?

Brack. Frankly, yes.

Hedda. Now you make me really curious—

Brack. Do you know where he and one or two of the others finished the night, Mrs. Hedda?

Hedda. If it is not quite unmentionable, tell me.

Brack. Oh no, it's not at all unmentionable. Well, they put in an appearance at a particularly animated soiree.

Hedda. Of the lively kind?

Brack. Of the very liveliest—

Hedda. Tell me more of this, Judge Brack—

Brack. Lovborg, as well as the others, had been invited in advance. I knew all about it. But he had declined the invitation; for now, as you know, he has become a new man.

Hedda. Up at the Elvsteds', yes. But he went after all, then?

Brack. Well, you see, Mrs. Hedda—unhappily the spirit moved him at my rooms last evening—

Hedda. Yes, I hear he found inspiration.

Brack. Pretty violent inspiration. Well, I fancy that altered his purpose; for we menfolk are unfortunately not always so firm in our principles as we ought to be.

Hedda. Oh, I am sure you are an exception, Judge Brack. But as to Lovborg—?

Brack. To make a long story short—he landed at last in Mademoiselle Diana's rooms.

Hedda. Mademoiselle Diana's?

Brack. It was Mademoiselle Diana that was giving the soiree, to a select circle of her admirers and her lady friends.

Hedda. Is she a red-haired woman?

Brack. Precisely.

Hedda. A sort of a—singer?

Brack. Oh yes—in her leisure moments. And moreover a mighty huntress—of men—Mrs. Hedda. You have no doubt heard of her. Eilert Lovborg was one of her most enthusiastic protectors—in the days of his glory.

Hedda. And how did all this end?

Brack. Far from amicably, it appears. After a most tender meeting, they seem to have come to blows—

Hedda. Lovborg and she?

Brack. Yes. He accused her or her friends of having robbed him. He declared that his pocket-book had disappeared—and other things as well. In short, he seems to have made a furious disturbance.

Hedda. And what came of it all?

Brack. It came to a general scrimmage, in which the ladies as well as the gentlemen took part. Fortunately the police at last appeared on the scene.

Hedda. The police too?

Brack. Yes. I fancy it will prove a costly frolic for Eilert Lovborg, crazy being that he is.

Hedda. How so?

Brack. He seems to have made a violent resistance—to have hit one of the constables on the head and torn the coat off his back. So they had to march him off to the police-station with the rest.

Hedda. How have you learnt all this?

Brack. From the police themselves.

Hedda. [*Gazing straight before her.*] So that is what happened. Then he had no vine-leaves in his hair.

Brack. Vine-leaves, Mrs. Hedda?

Hedda. [*Changing her tone.*] But tell me now, Judge—what is your real reason for tracking out Eilert Lovborg's movements so carefully?

Brack. In the first place, it could not be entirely indifferent to me if it should appear in the police-court that he came straight from my house.

Hedda. Will the matter come into court then?

Brack. Of course. However, I should scarcely have troubled so much about that. But I thought that, as a friend of the family, it was my duty to supply you and Tesman with a full account of his nocturnal exploits.

Hedda. Why so, Judge Brack?

Brack. Why, because I have a shrewd suspicion that he intends to use you as a sort of blind.

Hedda. Oh, how can you think such a thing!

Brack. Good heavens, Mrs. Hedda—we have eyes in our head. Mark my words! This Mrs. Elvsted will be in no hurry to leave town again.

Hedda. Well, even if there should be anything between them, I suppose there are plenty of other places where they could meet.

Brack. Not a single home. Henceforth, as before, every respectable house will be closed against Eilert Lovborg.

Hedda. And so ought mine to be, you mean?

Brack. Yes. I confess it would be more than painful to me if this personage were to be made free of your house. How superfluous, how intrusive, he would be, if he were to force his way into—

Hedda. —into the triangle?

Brack. Precisely. It would simply mean that I should find myself homeless.

Hedda. [*Looks at him with a smile.*] So you want to be the one cock in the basket[1]—that is your aim.

Brack. [*Nods slowly and lowers his voice.*] Yes, that is my aim. And for that I will fight—with every weapon I can command.

Hedda. [*Her smile vanishing.*] I see you are a dangerous person—when it comes to the point.

Brack. Do you think so?

Hedda. I am beginning to think so. And I am exceedingly glad to think—that you have no sort of hold over me.

Brack. [*Laughing equivocally.*] Well well, Mrs. Hedda—perhaps you are right there. If I had, who knows what I might be capable of?

Hedda. Come come now, Judge Brack! That sounds almost like a threat.

Brack. [*Rising.*] Oh, not at all! The triangle, you know, ought, if possible, to be spontaneously constructed.

Hedda. There I agree with you.

Brack. Well, now I have said all I had to say; and I had better be getting back to town. Good-bye, Mrs. Hedda. [*He goes towards the glass door.*]

Hedda. [*Rising.*] Are you going through the garden?

Brack. Yes, it's a short cut for me.

Hedda. And then it is a back way, too.

Brack. Quite so. I have no objection to back ways. They may be piquant enough at times.

Hedda. When there is ball practice going on, you mean?

Brack. [*In the doorway, laughing to her.*] Oh, people don't shoot their tame poultry, I fancy.

Hedda. [*Also laughing.*] Oh no, when there is only one cock in the basket—

[*They exchange laughing nods of farewell. He goes. She closes the door behind him.*

HEDDA, who has become quite serious, stands for a moment looking out. Presently she goes and peeps through the curtain over the middle doorway. Then she goes to the writing-table, takes LOVBORG'S packet out of the bookcase, and is on the point of looking through its contents. BERTA is heard speaking loudly in the hall. HEDDA turns and listens. Then she hastily locks up the packet in the drawer, and lays the key on the inkstand.

EILERT LOVBORG, with his greatcoat on and his hat in his hand, tears open the hall door. He looks somewhat confused and irritated.]

Lovborg. [*Looking towards the hall.*] and I tell you I must and will come in! There!

[He closes the door, turns, sees HEDDA, at once regains his self-control, and bows.]

Hedda. [*At the writing-table.*] Well, Mr Lovborg, this is rather a late hour to call for Thea.

Lovborg. You mean rather an early hour to call on you. Pray pardon me.

Hedda. How do you know that she is still here?

Lovborg. They told me at her lodgings that she had been out all night.

Hedda. [*Going to the oval table.*] Did you notice anything about the people of the house when they said that?

Lovborg. [*Looks inquiringly at her.*] Notice anything about them?

Hedda. I mean, did they seem to think it odd?

Lovborg. [*Suddenly understanding.*] Oh yes, of course! I am dragging her down with me! However, I didn't notice anything.—I suppose Tesman is not up yet.

Hedda. No—I think not—

Lovborg. When did he come home?

Hedda. Very late.

Lovborg. Did he tell you anything?

Hedda. Yes, I gathered that you had had an exceedingly jolly evening at Judge Brack's.

Lovborg. Nothing more?

Hedda. I don't think so. However, I was so dreadfully sleepy—

[*MRS. ELVSTED enters through the curtains of the middle doorway.*]

Mrs. Elvsted. [*Going towards him.*] Ah, Lovborg! At last—!

Lovborg. Yes, at last. And too late!

Mrs. Elvsted. [*Looks anxiously at him.*] What is too late?

Lovborg. Everything is too late now. It is all over with me.

Mrs. Elvsted. Oh no, no—don't say that!

Lovborg. You will say the same when you hear—

Mrs. Elvsted. I won't hear anything!

Hedda. Perhaps you would prefer to talk to her alone? If so, I will leave you.

Lovborg. No, stay—you too. I beg you to stay.

Mrs. Elvsted. Yes, but I won't hear anything, I tell you.

Lovborg. It is not last night's adventures that I want to talk about.

Mrs. Elvsted. What is it then—?

Lovborg. I want to say that now our ways must part.

Mrs. Elvsted. Part!

Hedda. [*Involuntarily.*] I knew it!

Lovborg. You can be of no more service to me, Thea.

Mrs. Elvsted. How can you stand there and say that! No more service to you! Am I not to help you now, as before? Are we not to go on working together?

Lovborg. Henceforward I shall do no work.

Mrs. Elvsted. [*Despairingly.*] Then what am I to do with my life?

Lovborg. You must try to live your life as if you had never know me.

Mrs. Elvsted. But you know I cannot do that!

Lovborg. Try if you cannot, Thea. You must go home again—

Mrs. Elvsted. [*In vehement protest.*] Never in this world! Where you are, there will I be also! I will not let myself be driven away like this! I will remain here! I will be with you when the book appears.

Hedda. [*Half aloud, in suspense.*] Ah yes—the book!

Lovborg. [*Looks at her.*] My book and Thea's; for that is what it is.

Mrs. Elvsted. Yes, I feel that it is. And that is why I have a right to be with you when it appears! I will see with my own eyes how respect and honour pour in upon you afresh. And the happiness—the happiness—oh, I must share it with you!

Lovborg. Thea—our book will never appear.

Hedda. Ah!

Mrs. Elvsted. Never appear!

Lovborg. Can never appear.

Mrs. Elvsted. [*In agonised foreboding.*] Lovborg—what have you done with the manuscript?

Hedda. [*Looks anxiously at him.*] Yes, the manuscript—?

Mrs. Elvsted. Where is it?

Lovborg. The manuscript—. Well then—I have torn the manuscript into a thousand pieces.

Mrs. Elvsted. [*Shrieks.*] Oh no, no—!

Hedda. [*Involuntarily.*] But that's not—

Lovborg. [*Looks at her.*] Not true, you think?

Hedda. [*Collecting herself.*] Oh well, of course—since you say so. But it sounded so improbable—

Lovborg. It is true, all the same.

Mrs. Elvsted. [*Wringing her hands.*] Oh God—oh God, Hedda—torn his own work to pieces!

Lovborg. I have torn my own life to pieces. So why should I not tear my life-work too—?

Mrs. Elvsted. And you did this last night?

Lovborg. Yes, I tell you! Tore it into a thousand pieces—and scattered them on the fiord—far out. There there is cool sea-water at any rate—let them drift upon it—drift with the current and the wind. And then presently they will sink—deeper and deeper—as I shall, Thea.

Mrs. Elvsted. Do you know, Lovborg, that what you have done with the book—I shall think of it to my dying day as though you had killed a little child.

Lovborg. Yes, you are right. It is a sort of child-murder.

Mrs. Elvsted. How could you, then—! Did not the child belong to me too?

Hedda. [*Almost inaudibly.*] Ah, the child—

Mrs. Elvsted. [*Breathing heavily.*] It is all over then. Well well, now I will go, Hedda.

Hedda. But you are not going away from town?

Mrs. Elvsted. Oh, I don't know what I shall do. I see nothing but darkness before me. [She goes out by the hall door.

Hedda. [*Stands waiting for a moment.*] So you are not going to see her home, Mr. Lovborg?

Lovborg. I? Through the streets? Would you have people see her walking with me?

Hedda. Of course I don't know what else may have happened last night. But is it so utterly irretrievable?

Lovborg. It will not end with last night—I know that perfectly well. And the thing is that now I have no taste for that sort of life either. I won't begin it anew. She has broken my courage and my power of braving life out.

Hedda. [*Looking straight before her.*] So that pretty little fool has had her fingers in a man's destiny. [*Looks at him.*] But all the same, how could you treat her so heartlessly.

Lovborg. Oh, don't say that I was heartless!

Hedda. To go and destroy what has filled her whole soul for months and years! You do not call that heartless!

Lovborg. To you I can tell the truth, Hedda.

Hedda. The truth?

Lovborg. First promise me—give me your word—that what I now confide in you Thea shall never know.

Hedda. I give you my word.

Lovborg. Good. Then let me tell you that what I said just now was untrue.

Hedda. About the manuscript?

Lovborg. Yes. I have not torn it to pieces—nor thrown it into the fiord.

Hedda. No, no—. But—where is it then?

Lovborg. I have destroyed it none the less—utterly destroyed it, Hedda!

Hedda. I don't understand.

Lovborg. Thea said that what I had done seemed to her like a child-murder.

Hedda. Yes, so she said.

Lovborg. But to kill his child—that is not the worst thing a father can do to it.

Hedda. Not the worst?

Lovborg. Suppose now, Hedda, that a man—in the small hours of the morning—came home to his child's mother after a night of riot and debauchery, and said: "Listen—I have been here and there—in this place and in that. And I have taken our child with—to this place and to that. And I have lost the child—utterly lost it. The devil knows into what hands it may have fallen—who may have had their clutches on it."

Hedda. Well—but when all is said and done, you know—this was only a book—

Lovborg. Thea's pure soul was in that book.

Hedda. Yes, so I understand.

Lovborg. And you can understand, too, that for her and me together no future is possible.

Hedda. What path do you mean to take then?

Lovborg. None. I will only try to make an end of it all—the sooner the better.

Hedda. [*A step nearer him.*] Eilert Lovborg—listen to me.—Will you not try to—to do it beautifully?

Lovborg. Beautifully? [*Smiling.*] With vine-leaves in my hair, as you used to dream in the old days—?

Hedda. No, no. I have lost my faith in the vine-leaves. But beautifully nevertheless! For once in a way!—Good-bye! You must go now—and do not come here any more.

Lovborg. Good-bye, Mrs. Tesman. And give George Tesman my love.

[*He is on the point of going.*]

Hedda.

No, wait! I must give you a memento to take with you.

[*She goes to the writing-table and opens the drawer and the pistol-case; then returns to LOVBORG with one of the pistols.*

Lovborg. [Looks at her.] This? Is this the memento?

Hedda. [Nodding slowly.] Do you recognise it? It was aimed at you once.

Lovborg. You should have used it then.

Hedda. Take it—and do you use it now.

Lovborg. [*Puts the pistol in his breast pocket.*] Thanks!

Hedda. And beautifully, Eilert Lovborg. Promise me that!

Lovborg. Good-bye, Hedda Gabler. [*He goes out by the hall door.*]

[*HEDDA listens for a moment at the door. Then she goes up to the writing-table, takes out the packet of manuscript, peeps under the cover, draws a few of the sheets half out, and looks at them. Next she goes over and seats herself in the arm-chair beside the stove, with the packet in her lap. Presently she opens the stove door, and then the packet.*]

Hedda. [*Throws one of the quires into the fire and whispers to herself.*] Now I am burning your child, Thea!—Burning it, curly-locks! [*Throwing one or two more quires into the stove.*] Your child and Eilert Lovborg's. [*Throws the rest in.*] I am burning—I am burning your child.

---

1. *"Enest hane i kurven"*—a proverbial saying.

ACT FOURTH

SCENE: The same rooms at the TESMANS'. It is evening. The drawing-room is in darkness. The back room is light by the hanging lamp over the table. The curtains over the glass door are drawn close.

HEDDA, dressed in black, walks to and fro in the dark room. Then she goes into the back room and disappears for a moment to the left. She is heard to strike a few chords on the piano. Presently she comes in sight again, and returns to the drawing-room.

BERTA enters from the right, through the inner room, with a lighted lamp, which she places on the table in front of the corner settee in the drawing-room. Her eyes are red with weeping, and she has black ribbons in her cap. She goes quietly and circumspectly out to the right. HEDDA goes up to the glass door, lifts the curtain a little aside, and looks out into the darkness.

Shortly afterwards, MISS TESMAN, in mourning, with a bonnet and veil on, comes in from the hall. HEDDA goes towards her and holds out her hand.

Miss Tesman. Yes, Hedda, here I am, in mourning and forlorn; for now my poor sister has at last found peace.

Hedda. I have heard the news already, as you see. Tesman sent me a card.

Miss Tesman. Yes, he promised me he would. But nevertheless I thought that to Hedda—here in the house of life—I ought myself to bring the tidings of death.

83

Hedda. That was very kind of you.

Miss Tesman. Ah, Rina ought not to have left us just now. This is not the time for Hedda's house to be a house of mourning.

Hedda. [*Changing the subject.*] She died quite peacefully, did she not, Miss Tesman?

Miss Tesman. Oh, her end was so calm, so beautiful. And then she had the unspeakable happiness of seeing George once more—and bidding him good-bye.—Has he not come home yet?

Hedda. No. He wrote that he might be detained. But won't you sit down?

Miss Tesman. No thank you, my dear, dear Hedda. I should like to, but I have so much to do. I must prepare my dear one for her rest as well as I can. She shall go to her grave looking her best.

Hedda. Can I not help you in any way?

Miss Tesman. Oh, you must not think of it! Hedda Tesman must have no hand in such mournful work. Nor let her thought dwell on it either—not at this time.

Hedda. One is not always mistress of one's thoughts—

Miss Tesman. [*Continuing.*] Ah yes, it is the way of the world. At home we shall be sewing a shroud; and here there will soon be sewing too, I suppose—but of another sort, thank God!

[*GEORGE TESMAN enters by the hall door.*]

Hedda. Ah, you have come at last!

Tesman. You here, Aunt Julia? With Hedda? Fancy that!

Miss Tesman. I was just going, my dear boy. Well, have you done all you promised?

Tesman. No; I'm really afraid I have forgotten half of it. I must come to you again to-morrow. To-day my brain is all in a whirl. I can't keep my thoughts together.

Miss Tesman. Why, my dear George, you mustn't take it in this way.

Tesman. Mustn't—? How do you mean?

Miss Tesman. Even in your sorrow you must rejoice, as I do—rejoice that she is at rest.

Tesman. Oh yes, yes—you are thinking of Aunt Rina.

Hedda. You will feel lonely now, Miss Tesman.

Miss Tesman. Just at first, yes. But that will not last very long, I hope. I daresay I shall soon find an occupant for Rina's little room.

Tesman. Indeed? Who do you think will take it? Eh?

Miss Tesman. Oh, there's always some poor invalid or other in want of nursing, unfortunately.

Hedda. Would you really take such a burden upon you again?

Miss Tesman. A burden! Heaven forgive you, child—it has been no burden to me.

Hedda. But suppose you had a total stranger on your hands—

Miss Tesman. Oh, one soon makes friends with sick folk; and it's such an absolute necessity for me to have some one to live for. Well, heaven be praised, there may soon be something in this house, too, to keep an old aunt busy.

Hedda. Oh, don't trouble about anything here.

Tesman. Yes, just fancy what a nice time we three might have together, if—?

Hedda. If—?

Tesman. [*Uneasily.*] Oh nothing. It will all come right. Let us hope so—eh?

Miss Tesman. Well well, I daresay you two want to talk to each other. [*Smiling.*] And perhaps Hedda may have something to tell you too, George. Good-bye! I must go home to Rina. [*Turning at the door.*] How strange it is to think that now Rina is with me and with my poor brother as well!

Tesman. Yes, fancy that, Aunt Julia! Eh?

[*MISS TESMAN goes out by the hall door.*]

Hedda. [*Follows TESMAN coldly and searchingly with her eyes.*] I almost believe your Aunt Rina's death affects you more than it does your Aunt Julia.

Tesman. Oh, it's not that alone. It's Eilert I am so terribly uneasy about.

Hedda. [*Quickly.*] Is there anything new about him?

Tesman. I looked in at his rooms this afternoon, intending to tell him the manuscript was in safe keeping.

Hedda. Well, did you find him?

Tesman. No. He wasn't at home. But afterwards I met Mrs. Elvsted, and she told me that he had been here early this morning.

Hedda. Yes, directly after you had gone.

Tesman. And he said that he had torn his manuscript to pieces—eh?

Hedda. Yes, so he declared.

Tesman. Why, good heavens, he must have been completely out of his mind! And I suppose you thought it best not to give it back to him, Hedda?

Hedda. No, he did not get it.

Tesman. But of course you told him that we had it?

Hedda. No. [*Quickly.*] Did you tell Mrs. Elvsted?

Tesman. No; I thought I had better not. But you ought to have told him. Fancy, if, in desperation, he should go and do himself some injury! Let me have the manuscript, Hedda! I will take it to him at once. Where is it?

Hedda. [*Cold and immovable, leaning on the arm-chair.*] I have not got it.

Tesman. Have not got it? What in the world do you mean?

Hedda. I have burnt it—every line of it.

Tesman. [*With a violent movement of terror.*] Burnt! Burnt Eilert's manuscript!

Hedda. Don't scream so. The servant might hear you.

Tesman. Burnt! Why, good God—! No, no, no! It's impossible!

Hedda. It is so, nevertheless.

Tesman. Do you know what you have done, Hedda? It's unlawful appropriation of lost property. Fancy that! Just ask Judge Brack, and he'll tell you what it is.

Hedda. I advise you not to speak of it—either to Judge Brack or to anyone else.

Tesman. But how could you do anything so unheard-of? What put it into your head? What possessed you? Answer me that—eh?

Hedda. [*Suppressing an almost imperceptible smile.*] I did it for your sake, George.

Tesman. For my sake!

Hedda. This morning, when you told me about what he had read to you—

Tesman. Yes yes—what then?

Hedda. You acknowledged that you envied him his work.

Tesman. Oh, of course I didn't mean that literally.

Hedda. No matter—I could not bear the idea that any one should throw you into the shade.

Tesman. [*In an outburst of mingled doubt and joy.*] Hedda! Oh, is this true? But—but—I never knew you show your love like that before. Fancy that!

Hedda. Well, I may as well tell you that—just at this time— [*Impatiently breaking off.*] No, no; you can ask Aunt Julia. She well tell you, fast enough.

Tesman. Oh, I almost think I understand you, Hedda! [*Clasps his hands together.*] Great heavens! do you really mean it! Eh?

Hedda. Don't shout so. The servant might hear.

Tesman. [*Laughing in irrepressible glee.*] The servant! Why, how absurd you are, Hedda. It's only my old Berta! Why, I'll tell Berta myself.

Hedda. [*Clenching her hands together in desperation.*] Oh, it is killing me, —it is killing me, all this!

Tesman. What is, Hedda? Eh?

Hedda. [*Coldly, controlling herself.*] All this—absurdity—George.

Tesman. Absurdity! Do you see anything absurd in my being overjoyed at the news! But after all—perhaps I had better not say anything to Berta.

Hedda. Oh—why not that too?

Tesman. No, no, not yet! But I must certainly tell Aunt Julia. And then that you have begun to call me George too! Fancy that! Oh, Aunt Julia will be so happy—so happy!

Hedda. When she hears that I have burnt Eilert Lovborg's manuscript —for your sake?

Tesman. No, by-the-bye—that affair of the manuscript—of course nobody must know about that. But that you love me so much,[1] Hedda—Aunt Julia must really share my joy in that! I wonder, now, whether this sort of thing is usual in young wives? Eh?

Hedda. I think you had better ask Aunt Julia that question too.

Tesman. I will indeed, some time or other. [Looks uneasy and downcast again.] And yet the manuscript—the manuscript! Good God! it is terrible to think what will become of poor Eilert now.

[*MRS. ELVSTED, dressed as in the first Act, with hat and cloak, enters by the hall door.*]

Mrs. Elvsted. [*Greets them hurriedly, and says in evident agitation.*] Oh, dear Hedda, forgive my coming again.

Hedda. What is the matter with you, Thea?

Tesman. Something about Eilert Lovborg again—eh?

Mrs. Elvsted. Yes! I am dreadfully afraid some misfortune has happened to him.

Hedda. [*Seized her arm.*] Ah,—do you think so?

Tesman. Why, good Lord—what makes you think that, Mrs. Elvsted?

Mrs. Elvsted. I heard them talking of him at my boarding-house—just as I came in. Oh, the most incredible rumours are afloat about him to-day.

Tesman. Yes, fancy, so I heard too! And I can bear witness that he went straight home to bed last night. Fancy that!

Hedda. Well, what did they say at the boarding-house?

Mrs. Elvsted. Oh, I couldn't make out anything clearly. Either they knew nothing definite, or else—. They stopped talking when the saw me; and I did not dare to ask.

Tesman. [*Moving about uneasily.*] We must hope—we must hope that you misunderstood them, Mrs. Elvsted.

Mrs. Elvsted. No, no; I am sure it was of him they were talking. And I heard something about the hospital or—

Tesman. The hospital?

Hedda. No—surely that cannot be!

Mrs. Elvsted. Oh, I was in such mortal terror! I went to his lodgings and asked for him there.

Hedda. You could make up your mind to that, Thea!

Mrs. Elvsted. What else could I do? I really could bear the suspense no longer.

Tesman. But you didn't find him either—eh?

Mrs. Elvsted. No. And the people knew nothing about him. He hadn't been home since yesterday afternoon, they said.

Tesman. Yesterday! Fancy, how could they say that?

Mrs. Elvsted. Oh, I am sure something terrible must have happened to him.

Tesman. Hedda dear—how would it be if I were to go and make inquiries—?

Hedda. No, no—don't you mix yourself up in this affair.

[*JUDGE BRACK, with his hat in his hand, enters by the hall door, which BERTA opens, and closes behind him. He looks grave and bows in silence.*]

Tesman. Oh, is that you, my dear Judge? Eh?

Brack. Yes. It was imperative I should see you this evening.

Tesman. I can see you have heard the news about Aunt Rina?

Brack. Yes, that among other things.

Tesman. Isn't it sad—eh?

Brack. Well, my dear Tesman, that depends on how you look at it.

Tesman. [*Looks doubtfully at him.*] Has anything else happened?

Brack. Yes.

Hedda. [*In suspense.*] Anything sad, Judge Brack?

Brack. That, too, depends on how you look at it, Mrs. Tesman.

Mrs. Elvsted. [*Unable to restrain her anxiety.*] Oh! it is something about Eilert Lovborg!

Brack. [*With a glance at her.*] What makes you think that, Madam? Perhaps you have already heard something—?

Mrs. Elvsted. [*In confusion.*] No, nothing at all, but—

Tesman. Oh, for heaven's sake, tell us!

Brack. [*Shrugging his shoulders.*] Well, I regret to say Eilert Lovborg has been taken to the hospital. He is lying at the point of death.

Mrs. Elvsted. [*Shrieks.*] Oh God! oh God—!

Tesman. To the hospital! And at the point of death!

Hedda. [*Involuntarily.*] So soon then—

Mrs. Elvsted. [*Wailing.*] And we parted in anger, Hedda!

Hedda. [*Whispers.*] Thea—Thea—be careful!

Mrs. Elvsted. [*Not heeding her.*] I must go to him! I must see him alive!

Brack. It is useless, Madam. No one will be admitted.

Mrs. Elvsted. Oh, at least tell me what has happened to him? What is it?

Tesman. You don't mean to say that he has himself—Eh?

Hedda. Yes, I am sure he has.

Brack. [*Keeping his eyes fixed upon her.*] Unfortunately you have guessed quite correctly, Mrs. Tesman.

Mrs. Elvsted. Oh, how horrible!

Tesman. Himself, then! Fancy that!

Hedda. Shot himself!

Brack. Rightly guessed again, Mrs. Tesman.

Mrs. Elvsted. [*With an effort at self-control.*] When did it happen, Mr. Brack?

Brack. This afternoon—between three and four.

Tesman. But, good Lord, where did he do it? Eh?

Brack. [*With some hesitation.*] Where? Well—I suppose at his lodgings.

Mrs. Elvsted. No, that cannot be; for I was there between six and seven.

Brack. Well then, somewhere else. I don't know exactly. I only know that he was found—. He had shot himself—in the breast.

Mrs. Elvsted. Oh, how terrible! That he should die like that!

Hedda. [*To BRACK.*] Was it in the breast?

Brack. Yes—as I told you.

Hedda. Not in the temple?

Brack. In the breast, Mrs. Tesman.

Hedda. Well, well—the breast is a good place, too.

Brack. How do you mean, Mrs. Tesman?

Hedda. [*Evasively.*] Oh, nothing—nothing.

Tesman. And the wound is dangerous, you say—eh?

Brack. Absolutely mortal. The end has probably come by this time.

Mrs. Elvsted. Yes, yes, I feel it. The end! The end! Oh, Hedda—!

Tesman. But tell me, how have you learnt all this?

Brack. [*Curtly.*] Through one of the police. A man I had some business with.

Hedda. [*In a clear voice.*] At last a deed worth doing!

Tesman. [*Terrified.*] Good heavens, Hedda! what are you saying?

Hedda. I say there is beauty in this.

Brack. H'm, Mrs. Tesman—

Mrs. Elvsted. Oh, Hedda, how can you talk of beauty in such an act!

Hedda. Eilert Lovborg has himself made up his account with life. He has had the courage to do—the one right thing.

Mrs. Elvsted. No, you must never think that was how it happened! It must have been in delirium that he did it.

Tesman. In despair!

Hedda. That he did not. I am certain of that.

Mrs. Elvsted. Yes, yes! In delirium! Just as when he tore up our manuscript.

Brack. [*Starting.*] The manuscript? Has he torn that up?

Mrs. Elvsted. Yes, last night.

Tesman. [*Whispers softly.*] Oh, Hedda, we shall never get over this.

Brack. H'm, very extraordinary.

Tesman. [*Moving about the room.*] To think of Eilert going out of the world in this way! And not leaving behind him the book that would have immortalised his name—

Mrs. Elvsted. Oh, if only it could be put together again!

Tesman. Yes, if it only could! I don't know what I would not give—

Mrs. Elvsted. Perhaps it can, Mr. Tesman.

Tesman. What do you mean?

Mrs. Elvsted. [*Searches in the pocket of her dress.*] Look here. I have kept all the loose notes he used to dictate from.

Hedda. [*A step forward.*] Ah—!

Tesman. You have kept them, Mrs. Elvsted! Eh?

Mrs. Elvsted. Yes, I have them here. I put them in my pocket when I left home. Here they still are—

Tesman. Oh, do let me see them!

Mrs. Elvsted. [*Hands him a bundle of papers.*] But they are in such disorder—all mixed up.

Tesman. Fancy, if we could make something out of them, after all! Perhaps if we two put our heads together—

Mrs. Elvsted. Oh yes, at least let us try—

Tesman. We will manage it! We must! I will dedicate my life to this task.

Hedda. You, George? Your life?

Tesman. Yes, or rather all the time I can spare. My own collections must wait in the meantime. Hedda—you understand, eh? I owe this to Eilert's memory.

Hedda. Perhaps.

Tesman. And so, my dear Mrs. Elvsted, we will give our whole minds to it. There is no use in brooding over what can't be undone—eh? We must try to control our grief as much as possible, and—

Mrs. Elvsted. Yes, yes, Mr. Tesman, I will do the best I can.

Tesman. Well then, come here. I can't rest until we have looked through the notes. Where shall we sit? Here? No, in there, in the back room. Excuse me, my dear Judge. Come with me, Mrs. Elvsted.

Mrs. Elvsted. Oh, if only it were possible!

[*TESMAN and MRS. ELVSTED go into the back room. She takes off her hat and cloak. They both sit at the table under the hanging lamp, and are soon deep in an eager examination of the papers. HEDDA crosses to the stove and sits in the arm-chair. Presently BRACK goes up to her.*]

Hedda. [*In a low voice.*] Oh, what a sense of freedom it gives one, this act of Eilert Lovborg's.

Brack. Freedom, Mrs. Hedda? Well, of course, it is a release for him—

Hedda. I mean for me. It gives me a sense of freedom to know that a deed of deliberate courage is still possible in this world,—a deed of spontaneous beauty.

Brack. [*Smiling.*] H'm—my dear Mrs. Hedda—

Hedda. Oh, I know what you are going to say. For you are a kind of specialist too, like—you know!

Brack. [*Looking hard at her.*] Eilert Lovborg was more to you than perhaps you are willing to admit to yourself. Am I wrong?

Hedda. I don't answer such questions. I only know that Eilert Lovborg has had the courage to live his life after his own fashion. And then—the last great act, with its beauty! Ah! that he should have the will and the strength to turn away from the banquet of life—so early.

Brack. I am sorry, Mrs. Hedda,—but I fear I must dispel an amiable illusion.

Hedda. Illusion?

Brack. Which could not have lasted long in any case.

Hedda. What do you mean?

Brack. Eilert Lovborg did not shoot himself—voluntarily.

Hedda. Not voluntarily?

Brack. No. The thing did not happen exactly as I told it.

Hedda. [*In suspense.*] Have you concealed something? What is it?

Brack. For poor Mrs. Elvsted's sake I idealised the facts a little.

Hedda. What are the facts?

Brack. First, that he is already dead.

Hedda. At the hospital?

Brack. Yes—without regaining consciousness.

Hedda. What more have you concealed?

Brack. This—the event did not happen at his lodgings.

Hedda. Oh, that can make no difference.

Brack. Perhaps it may. For I must tell you—Eilert Lovborg was found shot in—in Mademoiselle Diana's boudoir.

Hedda. [*Makes a motion as if to rise, but sinks back again.*] That is impossible, Judge Brack! He cannot have been there again to-day.

Brack. He was there this afternoon. He went there, he said, to demand the return of something which they had taken from him. Talked wildly about a lost child—

Hedda. Ah—so that is why—

Brack. I thought probably he meant his manuscript; but now I hear he destroyed that himself. So I suppose it must have been his pocket-book.

Hedda. Yes, no doubt. And there—there he was found?

Brack. Yes, there. With a pistol in his breast-pocket, discharged. The ball had lodged in a vital part.

Hedda. In the breast—yes?

Brack. No—in the bowels.

Hedda. [*Looks up at him with an expression of loathing.*] That too! Oh, what curse is it that makes everything I touch turn ludicrous and mean?

Brack. There is one point more, Mrs. Hedda—another disagreeable feature in the affair.

Hedda. And what is that?

Brack. The pistol he carried—

Hedda. [*Breathless.*] Well? What of it?

Brack. He must have stolen it.

Hedda. [*Leaps up.*] Stolen it! That is not true! He did not steal it!

Brack. No other explanation is possible. He must have stolen it—. Hush!

[*TESMAN and MRS. ELVSTED have risen from the table in the back-room, and come into the drawing-room.*]

Tesman. [*With the papers in both his hands.*] Hedda, dear, it is almost impossible to see under that lamp. Think of that!

Hedda. Yes, I am thinking.

Tesman. Would you mind our sitting at you writing-table—eh?

Hedda. If you like. [*Quickly.*] No, wait! Let me clear it first!

Tesman. Oh, you needn't trouble, Hedda. There is plenty of room.

Hedda. No no, let me clear it, I say! I will take these things in and put them on the piano. There!

[*She has drawn out an object, covered with sheet music, from*

under the bookcase, places several other pieces of music upon it, and carries the whole into the inner room, to the left. TESMAN lays the scraps of paper on the writing-table, and moves the lamp there from the corner table. He and Mrs. Elvsted sit down and proceed with their work. HEDDA returns.]

Hedda. [*Behind Mrs. Elvsted's chair, gently ruffling her hair.*] Well, my sweet Thea,—how goes it with Eilert Lovborg's monument?

Mrs. Elvsted. [*Looks dispiritedly up at her.*] Oh, it will be terribly hard to put in order.

Tesman. We must manage it. I am determined. And arranging other people's papers is just the work for me.

[*HEDDA goes over to the stove, and seats herself on one of the footstools. BRACK stands over her, leaning on the arm-chair.*]

Hedda. [*Whispers.*] What did you say about the pistol?

Brack. [*Softly.*] That he must have stolen it.

Hedda. Why stolen it?

Brack. Because every other explanation ought to be impossible, Mrs. Hedda.

Hedda. Indeed?

Brack. [*Glances at her.*] Of course Eilert Lovborg was here this morning. Was he not?

Hedda. Yes.

Brack. Were you alone with him?

Hedda. Part of the time.

Brack. Did you not leave the room whilst he was here?

Hedda. No.

Brack. Try to recollect. Were you not out of the room a moment?

Hedda. Yes, perhaps just a moment—out in the hall.

Brack. And where was you pistol-case during that time?

Hedda. I had it locked up in—

Brack. Well, Mrs. Hedda?

Hedda. The case stood there on the writing-table.

Brack. Have you looked since, to see whether both the pistols are there?

Hedda. No.

Brack. Well, you need not. I saw the pistol found in Lovborg's pocket, and I knew it at once as the one I had seen yesterday—and before, too.

Hedda. Have you it with you?

Brack. No; the police have it.

Hedda. What will the police do with it?

Brack. Search till they find the owner.

Hedda. Do you think they will succeed?

Brack. [*Bends over her and whispers.*] No, Hedda Gabler—not so long as I say nothing.

Hedda. [*Looks frightened at him.*] And if you do not say nothing,— what then?

Brack. [*Shrugs his shoulders.*] There is always the possibility that the pistol was stolen.

Hedda. [*Firmly.*] Death rather than that.

Brack. [*Smiling.*] People say such things—but they don't do them.

Hedda. [*Without replying.*] And supposing the pistol was not stolen, and the owner is discovered? What then?

Brack. Well, Hedda—then comes the scandal!

Hedda. The scandal!

Brack. Yes, the scandal—of which you are so mortally afraid. You will, of course, be brought before the court—both you and Mademoiselle Diana. She will have to explain how the thing happened—whether it was an accidental shot or murder. Did the pistol go off as he was trying to take it out of his pocket, to threaten her with? Or did she tear the pistol out of his hand, shoot him, and push it back into his pocket? That would be quite like her; for she is an able-bodied young person, this same Mademoiselle Diana.

Hedda. But *I* have nothing to do with all this repulsive business.

Brack. No. But you will have to answer the question: Why did you give Eilert the pistol? And what conclusions will people draw from the fact that you did give it to him?

Hedda. [*Lets her head sink.*] That is true. I did not think of that.

Brack. Well, fortunately, there is no danger, so long as I say nothing.

Hedda. [*Looks up at him.*] So I am in your power, Judge Brack. You have me at your beck and call, from this time forward.

Brack. [*Whispers softly.*] Dearest Hedda—believe me—I shall not abuse my advantage.

Hedda. I am in your power none the less. Subject to your will and your demands. A slave, a slave then! [*Rises impetuously.*] No, I cannot endure the thought of that! Never!

Brack. [*Looks half-mockingly at her.*] People generally get used to the inevitable.

Hedda. [*Returns his look.*] Yes, perhaps. [*She crosses to the writing-table. Suppressing an involuntary smile, she imitates TESMAN'S intonations.*] Well? Are you getting on, George? Eh?

Tesman. Heaven knows, dear. In any case it will be the work of months.

Hedda. [*As before.*] Fancy that! [Passes her hands softly through

Mrs. Elvsted's hair.] Doesn't it seem strange to you, Thea? Here are you sitting with Tesman—just as you used to sit with Eilert Lovborg?

Mrs. Elvsted. Ah, if I could only inspire your husband in the same way!

Hedda. Oh, that will come too—in time.

Tesman. Yes, do you know, Hedda—I really think I begin to feel something of the sort. But won't you go and sit with Brack again?

Hedda. Is there nothing I can do to help you two?

Tesman. No, nothing in the world. [Turning his head.] I trust to you to keep Hedda company, my dear Brack.

Brack. [*With a glance at HEDDA.*] With the very greatest of pleasure.

Hedda. Thanks. But I am tired this evening. I will go in and lie down a little on the sofa.

Tesman. Yes, do dear—eh?

[*HEDDA goes into the back room and draws the curtains. A short pause. Suddenly she is heard playing a wild dance on the piano.*]

Mrs. Elvsted. [*Starts from her chair.*] Oh—what is that?

Tesman. [*Runs to the doorway.*] Why, my dearest Hedda—don't play dance-music to-night! Just think of Aunt Rina! And of Eilert too!

Hedda. [*Puts her head out between the curtains.*] And of Aunt Julia. And of all the rest of them.—After this, I will be quiet. [*Closes the curtains again.*]

Tesman. [*At the writing-table.*] It's not good for her to see us at this distressing work. I'll tell you what, Mrs. Elvsted,—you shall take the empty room at Aunt Julia's, and then I will come over in the evenings, and we can sit and work there—eh?

Hedda. [*In the inner room.*] I hear what you are saying, Tesman. But how am *I* to get through the evenings out here?

Tesman. [*Turning over the papers.*] Oh, I daresay Judge Brack will be so kind as to look in now and then, even though I am out.

Brack. [*In the arm-chair, calls out gaily.*] Every blessed evening, with all the pleasure in life, Mrs. Tesman! We shall get on capitally together, we two!

Hedda. [*Speaking loud and clear.*] Yes, don't you flatter yourself we will, Judge Brack? Now that you are the one cock in the basket—

[*A shot is heard within. TESMAN, MRS. ELVSTED, and BRACK leap to their feet.*]

Tesman. Oh, now she is playing with those pistols again.

[*He throws back the curtains and runs in, followed by MRS. ELVSTED. HEDDA lies stretched on the sofa, lifeless. Confusion and cries. BERTA enters in alarm from the right.*]

Tesman. [*Shrieks to BRACK.*] Shot herself! Shot herself in the temple! Fancy that!

Brack. [*Half-fainting in the arm-chair.*] Good God!—people don't do such things.

---

1. Literally, "That you burn for me."

Made in the USA
Middletown, DE
03 March 2021